HAUNTED
FREDERICKSBURG

MICHELLE L. HAMILTON

Haunted
America

Published by Haunted America
A Division of The History Press
Charleston, SC
www.historypress.com

First published 2024

Manufactured in the United States

ISBN 9781467157001

Library of Congress Control Number: 2024938197

CONTENTS

ACKNOWLEDGEMENTS

Writing is a solitary endeavor, but to get to the point where a writer can put words on the page takes a lot of assistance from many people.

First, I would like to thank Kate Jenkins, acquisitions editor for The History Press and Arcadia Publishing. Without Kate, this book would not have been published. Kate has been a wonderful editor assisting me in the completion of this book. Abigail Fleming also provided her assistance as copyeditor.

I would also like to thank my parents, who were so supportive during the writing process. Especially to my mother, who braved snow and icy winds in January to get the pictures featured in this book. A huge thank-you must also be given to my three poodles—Belle, Rose and Violet—who sat on my lap while I wrote this book. They made sure that I finished the book on time but also had the forethought to remind me to take breaks.

Thank you to my friend and amazing paranormal researcher Alex Matsuo, who offered support while writing her own book. Leanna Renee Hieber also was a font of wisdom and support during this project. I am grateful to call both of you, my friends.

I also need to thank Pamela Kinney for sharing her investigation at Barnes & Noble. The Culpeper Paranormal Investigations were also very generous in sharing the evidence they collected at the Mary Washington House and the Rising Sun Tavern.

John and Debbie Grimes were also so supportive of me during this project and were always asking me how the process was going. I am so grateful that we met, and without you, we would not have three spoiled poodles.

Heather Meadows and Kristen Burns offered me support, and their insights on the manuscript were gratefully appreciated.

Thank you to Brendan Noble, John Daly and Hugh Meechan and all the other panelists and listeners of *The Sense Sphere*. I enjoy talking about and debating *Doctor Who* with you.

I also wish to thank all the people who offered their support and interest in the project. Thanks also to Daniel Hawkins, the manager of the Rising Sun Tavern, for offering his insight into the history of the building. I wish to thank Genevieve Bugay, the manager of the Hugh Mercer Apothecary Shop, and guide Margaret Matarese, who very generously shared their knowledge with me.

I wish to dedicate this book to the memory of my dear friend Gail Huneycutt-Iqbal. Gail and I used to spend hours discussing history and ghost stories and I know she would have been thrilled with this book.

Finally, I would like to thank my niece and nephew, Audrey and Wyatt—I am so proud of you, and I can't wait to see what the future holds for you.

If I have missed anyone, please accept my sincerest apologies.

Introduction

Before we begin our journey through the ghost stories of Fredericksburg, it is important that we briefly discuss the history of the region. The following survey is in no way a definitive history of Fredericksburg.

Sitting on the fall line of the Rappahannock River, Fredericksburg, Virginia, was officially founded in 1728 as a port city in the English colony of Virginia. Before the city was officially laid out, the land was the home of the Manahoac, a small group of Siouan-language Indigenous people. The Manahoac lived in small villages at the falls of the Rappahannock River. In 1608, English explorer John Smith traveled up the Rappahannock River and encountered the Manahoacs. For many Indigenous peoples, interaction with the English colonizers had a negative effect, and by the mid-seventeenth century, the Manahoacs had been decimated by illness and warfare.

The first English settlement in the Fredericksburg area was the establishment of a fort in 1676. Until the early eighteenth century, the area that would become Fredericksburg was the frontier of the Virginia colony. As planters moved into the region and established tobacco plantations, the need for a port city on the Rappahannock became necessary. The county of Spotsylvania was created in 1720. In 1728, Fredericksburg, named for Frederick, Prince of Wales, was declared the port city for Spotsylvania County. Additionally, town planners named many of the city's main streets for members of the Hanoverian dynasty. The county seat of Spotsylvania County was moved to Fredericksburg in 1732.

The city of Fredericksburg viewed from Chatham Manor. *Author's photo.*

During the colonial era, Fredericksburg was a bustling, vibrant port city. The economy of the region was based on the growing and cultivation of tobacco. Planters transported their tobacco crops to Fredericksburg, where they were inspected and purchased in tobacco counting houses. Armed with cash or script, planters would visit the shops and taverns, where merchants and tavernkeepers did their best to separate the planters from their money. While in Fredericksburg, planters could visit the theater, attend church at St. George's or bet on the outcome of a horse race. The wealth of the tobacco planters was built on chattel slavery. Slave traders sold human beings at public gatherings, including at the Fredericksburg market. During the eighteenth century, slave ships also docked at the Fredericksburg Harbor, offloading Africans to a life of hardship and misery.

Fredericksburg was the childhood home of George Washington, who visited the town frequently. Several members of the Washington family lived in Fredericksburg. During the American Revolution, Fredericksburg was of strategic importance as the location of a gun manufactory. Two Fredericksburg residents, Dr. Hugh Mercer and George Weedon, became generals in the Continental army. Even the father of America's navy,

Admiral John Paul Jones, briefly called Fredericksburg home in the 1770s. In 1781, Fredericksburg received a town charter and established its own court, council and mayor.

After the Revolutionary War, Fredericksburg continued to prosper with the establishment of mills along the Rappahannock River. The construction of a bridge across the Rappahannock River, along with a turnpike and plank roads, promoted trade and commerce throughout the region. The Richmond, Fredericksburg and Potomac Railroad opened in 1837 and connected the town to Richmond. During the antebellum era, the region continued to rely on slave labor as the keystone of the area's wealth.

The Civil War profoundly changed Fredericksburg and has left a mark that is still felt in the region today. During the war, ten thousand enslaved people passed through Fredericksburg seeking their freedom by crossing Union lines. The town was occupied eleven times by Union and Confederate forces, and many buildings in the area feature the graffiti the soldiers left behind. The Battle of Fredericksburg, fought on December 11–15, 1862, brought carnage and destruction to the town. At that time, the Battle of Fredericksburg was the largest engagement in American history. Out of the carnage of war, a hero emerged when Second Lieutenant Richard Rowland

The cemetery of St. George's Episcopal Church was created in 1728. *Author's photo*.

Kirkland of the Second South Carolina left the safety of the Confederate entrenchments to provide water to wounded Union and Confederate soldiers at Marye's Heights. Today, a monument stands at Marye's Heights to commemorate his compassion.

The horrors of the Civil War left Fredericksburg a shell of its former self. It would take nearly a century before the town fully recovered. Fredericksburg became an independent city in 1879 and separated from Spotsylvania County. Growth in Fredericksburg was further hampered by Jim Crow–era racial segregation. The civil rights movement put an end to legalized segregation, but the wounds from that era are still healing.

Today, Fredericksburg is a vibrant city and has become a popular tourist destination. People from across the nation and around the world visit Fredericksburg to learn about its history and sample the food of our eclectic mix of restaurants. With so much rich history, it is no wonder that Fredericksburg also has acquired its fair share of ghost stories. There have been stories about ghosts in Fredericksburg since before the Civil War. At times, it feels like practically every building in town has its own ghost story.

Graffiti from a Civil War soldier on the exterior of Aquia Episcopal Church. *Author's photo.*

The Richard Rowland Kirkland memorial commemorates Kirkland's bravery during the Battle of Fredericksburg when he brought water to wounded soldiers at Marye's Heights. *Author's photo.*

The purpose of this book is not to be the definitive account of every haunted site in Fredericksburg and the surrounding area. Ghost stories help us connect with the past on the human level. Traditional history records the dates of births, deaths, marriages and great events, but through ghost stories, the reader can connect with the emotions experienced by people from the past. The joys and sorrows of the past have embedded themselves into the fabric of the buildings and sites. These emotions can still be felt, particularly by those who are sensitive to the paranormal. The ghosts of Fredericksburg are a friendly bunch—in my research, I did not find any that were negative or wished harm on the living. Most of the paranormal activity that I uncovered seems to be residual in nature—a playback of what happened at the site. For the living, witnessing a residual haunt is like watching a movie: the person can see it but cannot interact with the film. The ghosts that appear to be intelligent, those that know that they are no longer living, appear to haunt their homes not necessarily because they have unfinished business but because they are still protecting their beloved home.

I have selected my favorite sites and the stories that I felt best illustrated the history of the region. In the following pages, I have tried to record the history of the sites to the best of my ability. As you will see, some details are difficult to accurately track down. Any mistakes that I have made are mine alone and do not reflect the owners or managers of the sites covered. The same can be said for the opinions that I have expressed about the sites and the possible identities of the ghosts mentioned. This book is meant to be used as a guide to the haunted history of Fredericksburg, but I must stress that readers should follow the rules and guidelines of each location. Please, do not trespass on any of the sites and respect the locations that are private homes.

1
MARY WASHINGTON HOUSE

A t 1200 Charles Street stands a large, white wood-sided house. This is
the Mary Washington House, the home where the mother of George
Washington lived for the final seventeen years of her life. The property
reflects the changes Fredericksburg experienced from the colonial era—
when the house consisted of a small three-room cottage with a detached
kitchen dependency—to its modern-day appearance. Today, visitors from
around the world come to learn about the history and heritage of the region.
Though time has passed, guests and staff of the Mary Washington House
can still encounter the spirits of its former occupants. Before we discuss the
paranormal activity that has occurred at the museum, we will start with the
history of the house and the life of Mary Washington.

Mary Ball Washington was born in 1708 in Lancaster County, Virginia,
to Joseph and Mary Johnson Ball. When Mary was three, her father died.
Joseph Ball bequeathed to his daughter land, cattle, household goods—
including enough feathers to make a bed—and three enslaved Black men.
At the age of three, Mary became an enslaver. This had a profound impact
on how she viewed her place in society as a member of the Virginia gentry.

Following Joseph's death, Mary's mother remarried. But by the time
Mary was thirteen, her stepfather and mother had both passed away,
leaving Mary an orphan. She was raised by her older half-sister Elizabeth
Bonum. A family friend, George Eskeridge, served as her legal advisor,
and according to tradition, it was Eskeridge who introduced Mary to her
husband, Augustine Washington.

The Mary Washington House was built in 1759 and was the home of Mary Ball Washington for the final seventeen years of her life. *Author's photo.*

Augustine Washington was a wealthy landowner whose first wife, Jane Butler Washington, had died, leaving him with a young daughter—also named Jane—to raise. Augustine Washington also had two older sons, Lawrence and Augustine Jr., who were attending Appleby Grammer School in England. Sometime in 1730, George Eskeridge introduced Mary to Augustine Washington. The couple began to court, and on March 6, 1731, they married. The couple started their family quickly; in February 1732, Mary gave birth to her first child, George. Mary would have five more children with her husband: Betty, Samuel, John Augustine, Charles and Mildred. Sadly, Jane and Mildred died in childhood.

By 1743, Mary was living at Ferry Farm with her husband and children. In the spring of that year, Augustine Washington fell ill with an unspecified stomach disorder and died after a brief illness. Mary was thirty-five years old and a widow with five children under the age of twelve to care for. With her husband's passing, Mary lost 60 percent of the income that she had relied on to raise her children. Per the inheritance laws of the period, a widow received the property (land and chattel) that she had brought to the marriage as part of her dowry. If there were children, her husband's estate would go to the surviving children.

Following Augustine's death, his larger properties of Little Hunting Creek (now known as Mount Vernon) and Pope's Creek (George Washington's birthplace) were inherited by Lawrence and Augustine Jr., along with the enslaved men, women and children who had been owned by their father. George Washington inherited from his father the plantation at Ferry Farm and enslaved people. Samuel, John Augustine and Charles received seven hundred acres of land that was divided between them along with enslaved people. Betty received £400 on her eighteenth birthday for her dowry and two enslaved women as her inheritance. From her husband, Mary received a life interest in the enslaved workers who would become the property of her children on her death.

Mary Washington could have remarried, as was common during the eighteenth century. But during the colonial era, per British Common Law, when a woman married, the money and property that she brought to the marriage as her dowry was given to her husband for him to control or sell as he saw fit. This included all money, land, household goods, farm animals and enslaved people. Because Mary was serving in trust for her minor children, meaning that she was supervising the handling of their inheritances, their property was included with their mother's property as part of her dowry until the boys reached twenty-one years old and Betty turned eighteen. That meant that if Mary chose to remarry, her husband could make improvements to the land, sell acreage and the enslaved workers and have control of the revenues from their properties until the boys were legally adults.

Augustine was concerned that his children could lose their inheritances and wrote in his will that his older sons, Lawrence and Augustine Jr., were to supervise the management of their half-brothers' estates. If they felt that Mary or her husband were not maintaining the boys' estates properly, they were to sue for custody and take George and his brothers away from their mother. Mary Washington could have lost custody of her children. She would not let that happen and decided to remain a widow and raise her children at Ferry Farm. As a widow in colonial Virginia, Mary had the freedom to manage her own affairs. Because the law viewed her as a single person, she could own property, own her own business, make contracts and purchase enslaved workers under her name.

Mary Washington raised her children at Ferry Farm and oversaw their education, which included lessons in social etiquette befitting their place as members of the Virginia gentry. As a teenager, George Washington borrowed money from his mother to take dancing lessons. George Washington left Ferry Farm at the age of sixteen to become a surveyor. He would never live at Ferry Farm again. At the age of nineteen, he joined the colonial militia, and after the death of his half-brother Lawrence, George moved to Mount Vernon. George rented Mount Vernon from Lawrence's widow. Following the death of his niece and his sister-in-law, George Washington inherited Mount Vernon, and he would live at the plantation for the remainder of his life. By the 1760s, George Washington had decided that he wanted to sell Ferry Farm, as the plantation had never been profitable. Mary Washington was still living at Ferry Farm and did not want to leave the farm to live with

A nineteenth-century artist's depiction of Mary Washington instructing her son George as a child. *Author's collection.*

one of her children and their families. At this time, it was rare for a single or widowed woman, particularly a member of the gentry who had a family, to live on her own. George agreed to not sell Ferry Farm and let his mother live on the property.

By the early 1770s, Mary Washington was in her early sixties and had lived twice the average life expectancy for a colonial woman. Her five surviving children had all married and moved away from Ferry Farm. Two of her children, Betty and Charles, were living in Fredericksburg. Mary's only surviving daughter, Betty, had married her distant cousin, the wealthy merchant Fielding Lewis. Fielding Lewis was overseeing the construction of his plantation, now known as Kenmore. Charles Washington, Mary's youngest son, lived on Caroline Street at the property that is now known as the Rising Sun Tavern. To visit her family and friends and to do business in Fredericksburg, Mary would have to cross the Rappahannock River using a ferryboat, which was dependent on the state of the river for safe crossing.

The winter of 1771–72 proved to be bitterly cold; during that winter, Mary fell ill with influenza. Her physicians, including Dr. Hugh Mercer, who treated her during her illness, were in Fredericksburg. Mary was not alone at Ferry Farm, as she was cared for by the labor of her enslaved workers, who cleaned her house, cooked her meals, tended the fields and cared for her beloved horses, including her favorite horse, called Shew Lace. Following her illness, Mary decided to move to Fredericksburg to be closer to her family. Instead of moving in with Betty or Charles, Mary requested her own house.

In accordance with her wishes, George Washington placed Ferry Farm up for sale and purchased property for his mother in Fredericksburg. "I did, at her request, but at my own expense, purchase a commodious house, garden and Lotts (of her own choosing) in Fredericksburg so that she might be near my Sister Lewis," George Washington wrote in 1781. The property that George purchased for his mother included a one-and-a-half-story three-room clapboard house that had been erected in 1759. The property included two half-acre lots with a detached kitchen and stable. Mary picked the property because it was next to her daughter and son-in-law. According to the Lewis children, Mary would frequently visit the Lewis family using a pathway that connected the properties.

Mary Washington moved into the house in April 1772 with six enslaved workers (three men and three women), three horses, two cows and a dog. She lived in the house for the final seventeen years of her life. During her time in Fredericksburg, Mary lived through the difficult days of the Revolutionary War. While she did not leave any documentation of her feelings about the

Revolutionary War, her grandchildren remembered her knitting socks for the soldiers and offering her blessings to Continental soldiers. Deeply religious, Mary attended St. George's Anglican (now Episcopal) Church. According to her grandchildren, Mary often visited an outcropping of rocks on the Kenmore Plantation to pray. This outcropping is now known as Meditation Rock and is where the Mary Washington Monument is located.

The original one-and-a-half-story cottage that Mary Washington lived in can be seen in the section of the house known as the Bed-Sitting Room and the room above it that is called the George Washington Bedroom. Renovations to the house have changed the room from the way it looked from 1772 to 1789. The Bed-Sitting Room was originally two rooms divided by a wall. One room was used for entertaining guests, and the other room was Mary Washington's bedchamber. The upstairs garret bedroom, now called the George Washington Room, was used for extra storage and as a guest room when George Washington spent the night. George Washington visited his mother frequently and, according to his diary, spent the night at the house six times.

In the room known today as the Bed-Sitting Room, Mary would have welcomed guests and entertained her family. Visitors included the Marquis de Lafayette, who met Mary in April 1781. For the remainder of Mary's life, Lafayette remained fond of Mary and mentioned her in his letters. "Rember me to Your Much Respected Mother—Her Happiness I Heartly Partake," Lafayette wrote to George Washington in 1783.

It was in that room that Mary saw George Washington for the last time. Washington had been elected president of United States and was settling his personal affairs before heading to New York City to be inaugurated. George knew that it would be the last time that he would see his mother alive; for several years, Mary had been fighting breast cancer. In March 1789, Washington came to Fredericksburg to say goodbye. According to family tradition, George asked his mother for her blessing, which she gave to her eldest son.

Mary Washington died of breast cancer on August 25, 1789, just before 3:00 p.m. Her death was reported worldwide, and her obituary was printed in newspapers, which was unusual at that time for a woman. On hearing the news of his mother's passing, George wrote to comfort his sister Betty: "Awful, and affecting as the death of a parent is, there is a consolation in knowing that Heaven has spared ours to an age, beyond which few attain." George mourned his mother's death by wearing a black mourning badge for five months. High-ranking members of the new government went into mourning for Mary Washington for five weeks as a sign of respect for the Washington family.

Without Mary Washington, the history of the United States would have been different. Mary kept George from joining the British navy, as she believed that it was a bad career move for her oldest son. She was correct: as a Virginian, George did not possess the money or connections to advance in the ranks. A cousin of George Washington wrote to a biographer in the nineteenth century about Mary: "Of the mother I was ten times more afraid than I ever was of my own parents. She awed me in the midst of her kindness, for she was, truly kind….I could not behold that remarkable woman without feelings it is impossible to describe." The highest praise for Mary Washington came from her son. In 1784, George Washington addressed the mayor and city council of Fredericksburg, and in his remarks, he praised his mother, declaring "My revered mother, by whose maternal hand, early deprived of a father I was led to manhood."

Following Mary Washington's death in 1789, her granddaughter Betty Lewis Carter moved into the house with her husband, Charles Carter, and the couple's five children. During the Carters' time in the house, they undertook extensive remodeling to the house, adding in a central hall, building an elegant parlor with hand-carved woodworking and raising the roof to create a second floor with additional sleeping quarters. While living in the house, Betty gave birth to three more children; sadly, two of the babies died as infants. The Carters resided at the house for only three years and moved out in 1793 to a plantation in Culpeper County.

The house went through several owners during the first decade of the nineteenth century. In 1806, Reverend Samuel B. Wilson, Fredericksburg's first Presbyterian minister, moved into the house. Along with raising a large family, Wilson operated a boys' school in the house. The addition of a school required further renovations to the house, and the north wing of the house was completed. This space was used as additional living and teaching spaces, as students also boarded at Wilson's school. After several years of operating the school, Wilson decided to cease operating the boys' school and opened a girls' school. This allowed Wilson to hire additional help, and two school mistresses were added to the staff. Due to financial difficulties, Reverend Wilson had to sell off the back lots that originally connected the property to Kenmore. Reverend Wilson and his family resided at the house for thirty-four years.

Following Reverend Wilson's occupation, the house was divided into the north and south wings and resembled a duplex. In 1855, Jane Dickenson purchased the house with two lots from Arthur A. Morson for $2,500. Jane Dickenson was a widow from Caroline County and moved to Fredericksburg with her children, grandchildren and enslaved workers. In 1860, Dickenson was fifty-five years old and resided in the house with her ten-year-old granddaughter Ellen B. Lewis. Dickenson and Ellen were cared for by the labor of six enslaved workers who ranged in age from eighteen to fifty-five years old.

The Civil War came to Fredericksburg in the summer of 1862 when the Union army occupied the town. During the Union occupation, many of Fredericksburg's enslaved population sought their freedom. It is unknown if Dickenson's enslaved workers were among those who fled the city. During the Battle of Fredericksburg in December 1862, Jane Dickenson was one of the few residents who remained in her home. According to Dickenson's great-granddaughter, "She was there during the dreadful Battle of Fredericksburg…and in the long upper-dormer windowed room, [she] nursed many of the wounded Confederate soldiers."

The Battle of Fredericksburg left its mark on the property, as the house was struck at least once by a Union cannonball. The ball struck the attic above the 1791 addition and passed through the rafters. By 1864, Jane Dickenson had left her home and hired a caretaker to protect the property. After the Battles of the Wilderness and Spotsylvania Court House, Fredericksburg was filled with wounded and dying Union soldiers. One such soldier was First Lieutenant Amos Rood of the Seventh Wisconsin Infantry, who had been seriously wounded when he was shot in the lung at the Battle of Spotsylvania Court House. Rood was first taken to Kenmore for treatment but realized that if he was to survive his injury, he had to find better accommodations. After wandering the streets of Fredericksburg, Rood found the Mary Washington House and convinced the housekeeper to let him in. Rood was able to begin his convalescence at the house and was moved by the fact that he was in the house that had belonged to the mother of George Washington. "I told my guests that if they could not recover here in such a sacred place, they couldn't get well anywhere!" Rood wrote in his memoirs.

Sometime during the war, the bodies of at least six Union soldiers were buried in the backyard of the Mary Washington House. After the war, during the Union occupation of Fredericksburg, Private Charles Fuchs/Fox of the Eleventh Connecticut fell ill and died on September 30, 1865. It is unclear where Fuchs was stationed in Fredericksburg, but following his death, he joined his comrades in the grave dug in the backyard of the Mary Washington House. Sadly, Fuchs is the only one of the six soldiers buried in the backyard to be positively identified. In 1866, Fuchs and his comrades were reinterred in the Fredericksburg National Cemetery, where he rests to this day in grave no. 2539.

In 1890, the Mary Washington House was saved from being dismantled and shipped to Chicago for the 1893 World Columbian Exposition. The Association for the Preservation of Virginia Antiquities raised $4,000 and saved the house. After being restored, the Mary Washington House opened as a museum in 1900. In 2012, the Washington Heritage Museums was founded and accepted the deed of gift from Preservation Virginia. Today, the Washington Heritage Museums maintains the Mary Washington House, the Rising Sun Tavern, the Hugh Mercer Apothecary Shop, the St. James House and the Mary Washington Monument and Monument Lodge.

Now that we have covered the history of the Mary Washington House, we can better understand the ghost stories connected to the site. It is not documented when the first paranormal activity was first experienced, but by the early 1970s, it was well known among the staff that something stirred in the house. In 1971, reporter Harold M. Farkas visited the Mary Washington House for a piece that he wrote for the *New York Times* about Virginia's "V.I.P. Ghosts." Farkas interviewed Gertude "Gertie" Sawyer, who was the "resident hostess" for the Mary Washington House. Sawyer managed the property and guides and lived on site as a full-time caretaker. She admitted that it took her a while to get used to living with unseen housemates.

Sawyer told the reporter that one winter morning, she "heard doors opening and closing and then the rustle of skirts." She was so frightened she fled the house. "I ran out of the house and spent the night with a friend," Sawyer admitted. Sawyer believed that she had had an encounter with the spirit of Mary Washington. Fortunately for Sawyer, she was able to make peace with living in a haunted building. She told Farkas that even though she had not actually seen the ghost of Mary Washington, she expected to see her any day. Despite

The sign of the Mary Washington House, where staff have heard a silk petticoat rustling in Mary Washington's bedroom. *Author's photo.*

being open to the idea that the house was haunted, Sawyer was concerned that the ghost stories would overshadow the history of the house. "The caretakers even say they have tried to tone down the ghost stories for fear of scaring off the help," Farkas wrote.

One of the most common reports at the Mary Washington House is of hearing the rustle of a skirt through the rooms. Typically, the sound is reported as silk petticoats rustling together. A few years ago, a guide reported to me that while she was sitting in the hallway between tours, she heard a silk petticoat rustling in the Bed-Sitting Room. She was sitting in the hallway with her chair facing the Bed-Sitting Room, when she looked up from her sewing, she said she saw the hem of a petticoat swish past the door. Did she catch sight of Mary Washington? The Bed-Sitting Room is the original section of the house where Mary lived for seventeen years. Several years ago, I permitted paranormal investigator Mike Ricksecker to investigate the house. During the investigation, he called psychic Vanessa Hogel to do a reading on the property. At the beginning of the call, Hogel did not know where Ricksecker was. One of the impressions that Hogel sensed was the sound of a rustling skirt.

Though I have not heard rustling petticoats, I have heard footsteps in the house. The most notable occasion was the day after Christmas 2020. Typically, the holiday season is a busy time for the museum, but 2020 had been a hard time for the site, as we were beginning to recover from the pandemic shutdown that had closed the museum for nine months. I was working as a tour guide that day with my dear friend and colleague Gail Huneycutt-Iqbal. We were just enjoying being in the house together after being separated for most of the year. The house was quiet, and we were reading in the front hallway when suddenly we heard a loud bang coming from upstairs. It sounded like something large had crashed to the floor. The sound was so loud it made us jump. Gail and I looked at each other, and we both laughed nervously. I was concerned that an artifact or the barrier in the George Washington Bedroom had fallen over. Realizing that I would have to go up to check, as I am the manager, I looked up at the ceiling and yelled, "I better not see anything when I get up there!" Steeling myself—as this was the only time, I was ever nervous to go upstairs by myself in the Mary Washington House—I went up to inspect the carnage that I expected to see. Instead of seeing smashed shards of antique pottery or a toppled barrier, I found everything as it should be. Nothing had been moved; nothing was out of place. I returned to my post and reported my findings to Gail. We just chuckled and shook our heads.

Less than forty-five minutes later, as we had just settled down from one unexpected occurrence, we both heard footsteps coming from the parlor. The footsteps sounded like the tread of a woman in heels. At the time, I had a pair of heeled shoes made in the style of the 1780s–'90s. The clip-clopping sound that we both heard sounded exactly like the noise French heels make on hardwood floors.

Paranormal activity at the Mary Washington House increases around Christmastime. In the eighteenth and nineteenth centuries, Christmas was a festive time when friends and family gathered. Several years ago, I was working as a guide at the house on December 23. It was the last day that the house would be open before the museum was closed for Christmas Eve and Christmas Day. I was the first person to arrive, and as I was going through the opening procedures, I kept hearing two men talking. No one was on the street outside the house, and I was completely alone. The voices were muffled, but it was clearly two men having a pleasant conversation. I was not afraid, even though I was alone. As the day progressed, the voices seemed to move throughout the house. When I first arrived, the voices were coming from the section of the house that is not open to the public. Later in the day, my coworker and I were in the museum store, and we heard the same voices coming from the front hallway. The voices were clearer, yet we could not make out what was being said. All that came across was that the tone was pleasant.

This is not the only time that voices have been heard in the house. In the fall of 2023, the gardener arrived at the house before the staff had arrived and entered the house to use the bathroom. While turning on the lights, he heard two women talking in the parlor. Like my previous encounter, he could not make out what they were saying, just that it was two women talking. The strangest voice that I heard in the house occurred the first winter I worked at the museum. I had been working as a guide for only a few weeks. I was standing in the front hall with my coworker and the house manager. We were chatting, as the day was dreary and there had not been any visitors. Suddenly, we all heard a man's voice speaking. We could not understand what he was saying, but it had the tone and inflection of a 1930s radio announcer. It was so strange that we all just brushed off what we had heard. Several years later, after I had become manager, I was in the museum's archives going through a scrapbook of newspaper clippings from the 1930s to the 1960s. I was looking for pieces that could be used for a display celebrating the fiftieth anniversary of the restoration of the Colonial Revival Garden. While leafing through the fragile scrapbook, I came across an article from 1932 about an NBC radio broadcast recorded in the Mary Washington House to commemorate the bicentennial of George Washington's birth. Had I heard a residual memory of that broadcast?

One of my favorite stories occurred in the summer of 2022. I was in the garden "weeding." I am not a gardener, and beyond a few common flowers, I am completely clueless in a garden. I had just returned from being out for over a week from a mild case of COVID, and the museum was between gardeners. It had been a rainy summer, so the greenery had sprouted everywhere. Being a hands-on manager, I was in the garden pulling what I thought were weeds. I was engrossed in my task and mentally enjoying pulling out pesky plants. I was attacking a patch of weeds when I heard a woman call my name. It was a clear voice, but it sounded like it had come from a distance. I looked up, but no one else was in the garden. I called out but got no response. I went and found my staff who were inside enjoying the A/C, and I asked if they were looking for me. They were not. I then went to the museum store to see if the volunteer in the shop had called my name. But the answer was the same; she had been busy restocking the shop and had not called for assistance. I then thought that maybe my boss had come from her office and had been looking for me.

Pulling out my cellphone, I called her, but she was still in her office offsite and had not been looking for me. Realizing that no one living had called for me, I then wondered if maybe I was pulling up the wrong thing. Later, when my boss came to the Mary Washington House, she confirmed that what I had been attacking so assiduously was in fact a medicinal plant—not a weed. I had attacked feverfew, a plant that was used in the colonial era to treat fevers, headaches and arthritis. Mary Washington was an avid gardener and would have grown and known the usages of medicinal plants. I felt that Mary Washington was stopping me from purging the garden of an important plant. From now on, when I pull weeds in the garden, I joke that I know I am pulling up weeds because I did not hear my name being called.

The funniest event that I witnessed during a paranormal investigation occurred during the summer of 2021. Paranormal researchers Alex Matsuo and Jason Scott Roach from the Association of Paranormal Research came to the Mary Washington House to investigate. I had been acquainted with Alex since I had moved to Virginia and liked her approach to the paranormal. It was a lovely summer evening, and midway through the investigation I took them to the second floor to investigate the George Washington Bedroom. We settled down on the floor, and Alex and Jason decided to conduct the Estes Method. The Estes Method was popularized at the Stanley Hotel in Estes Park, Colorado, and involves one participant placing a blindfold or eye mask over their eyes while listening to an SB7 Spirit Box and wearing headphones to block out external noise. The SB7 Spirit Box is a specially designed radio that scans AM and FM stations quickly. The theory is that ghosts can communicate through the white noise created by scanning the radio stations at a fast rate. The purpose of wearing the blindfold and headphones is to prevent the researcher from being influenced by the questions the other researchers ask during the experiment. The person who is selected to wear the headphones says whatever they hear.

Alex decided that she would be the person to listen to the Spirit Box; before settling in, she put out a cat toy as a trigger item. The cat toy was a ball that lit up when swatted by a cat's paw. Alex turned on the Spirit Box, put on her headphones and eye mask and closed her eyes. Jason and I started to ask a few innocuous questions. We were not getting much activity, and Jason decided to point out that if one of the spirits tapped the cat toy, it would light up. Suddenly, Alex interrupted our conversation with an indignant, "I am not a cat." Jason and I started laughing so hard I thought that we had ruined the investigation. Our laughter was interrupted again when Alex declared, "Don't say meow!" Following this declaration, our laughter reached a near ear-splitting level, and I was sure that Alex had heard us through her headphones.

After Jason and I had collected ourselves, we ended the Estes Method and tapped on Alex's leg to tell her to take off her eye mask and headphones. We asked her what she had heard. Alex answered that she had heard the voice of an adult woman saying that she was not a feline. Jason confirmed that after the first indignant response about not being a cat, he was going to make a meowing sound. Alex then relayed that after she had heard the woman say, "Don't say meow!" she had heard the woman laughing. We were all amused about what had happened, and this has become one of my favorite stories to tell during paranormal tours at the Mary Washington House.

Though Mary Washington's spirit is felt in the house, full-bodied apparitions are rare. A popular legend states that Mary's spirit has been seen walking the path that once connected the Mary Washington House to her daughter's residence at Kenmore. While this story is frequently recounted in books, I have never met a person who has seen the shade of Mary Washington walking through their property.

One intriguing story of a full-bodied apparition occurred in the garden of the Mary Washington House. This story was told to me by a former gardener. It occurred a few years before I was hired. It happened on a beautiful early summer evening. A man was walking his dog down Lewis

Street, which runs along the side of the Mary Washington House with a full view of the garden. It was a pleasant evening, just before twilight when it was getting cool but with enough light to safely walk without tripping in the dark. The man knew that the museum was closed and had never seen anyone at that hour on the property. As he passed the garden, he saw an older woman in colonial clothing bending over examining a flowerbed. He could not see her face, just that she was an older woman. His dog then started to bark at the woman. The man looked away from the woman to settle his dog. When he looked back to apologize to the woman for his dog's manners, the woman had disappeared.

Where the woman was standing, it would have been impossible for her to have disappeared that quickly, and the garden walkway in lined with gravel, so the man should have heard footsteps crunching if she had walked away. The man was puzzled and later inquired with the manager if the gardener wore period clothing while working in the garden. While the museum guides wear colonial attire, the Washington Heritage Museums does not require such period accuracy for the gardener. Could the man have seen the ghost of Mary Washington in her beloved garden? It's certainly possible, as contemporary accounts of Mary Washington during her time at the house documented that Mary spent most of her time in her garden. When Mary Washington met the Marquis de Lafayette in 1781, she was in her garden raking leaves.

While Mary Washington is the dominant spirit in her home and I like to joke that she is still supervising the staff to make sure that we are properly maintaining her house, she is not the only ghost believed to roam the halls. The spirits of the boys who attended Reverend Wilson's school are blamed for the mischievous pranks pulled on the staff and volunteers. One day before the museum store was moved to its present location, the volunteer gift shop buyer was using the Betsy Houston Room to sort her merchandise invoices. The Betsy Houston Room is not on public display and is used by the staff as a meeting room; the room was added onto the house in the 1840s. She had her invoices spread out neatly on the conference table when she was called away to assist a customer. When she returned to the room, the invoices had been scattered across the room like a mini tornado had swept through the space. She collected the invoices and had put them back in order when she was called away again. Upon her return to the room, the invoices had again been scattered. Exasperated, she scolded the boys to leave her invoices alone. Taking the message, her invoices were left alone.

The spirits of the enslaved workers who lived at the house are also felt. As a historian, I believe it is important to respectfully document and interpret the lives of everyone, free and enslaved, who lived on the property. One of the challenges of being a historian is to interpret the lives of those who did not leave written records. I can piece together part of their story through what is left in the writings of the Washington family, tax records and Mary Washington's will. Heartbreakingly, following Mary Washington's death in 1789, the six men and women she had enslaved were separated and given to six different members of the Washington family. They were ripped away from their family and friends and the place that they had called home for seventeen years. Though in life they were taken away from their loved ones, their spirits are still felt in the house. During a paranormal investigation, my mother was with the team while they were investigating the section of the house that was the original kitchen. The team was using a spirit box to communicate with the spirits. When it was my mother's turn to ask a question, she thanked Lydia, Old Bet, Little Bet, George, Frank and Tom for all the hard work they had done to care for the house and for nursing Mary when she was dying from breast cancer. She told them that they were remembered and that their story was being told. When she was finished, everyone could clearly hear a voice saying "thank you" coming from the Spirit Box.

The horrors of the Civil War are also still felt on the property. During a paranormal investigation conducted by paranormal researcher Alex Matsuo and Jason Scott Roach, the sound of a man speaking German was heard coming through the Echo Box. Could that have been the spirit of Charles Fuchs, who was born in Germany and had been buried in the garden following his death in 1865? A visiting medium told me that there was a Civil War soldier who haunted the museum. He has decided to stay and serve as a protector of the site because the staff and volunteers are predominantly women.

I encourage everyone to come and visit the Mary Washington House to learn about the life of a remarkable woman. Mary Washington was a single mother who encountered and overcame many challenges. Her strength of character was imparted to her son George Washington. At the Mary Washington House, visitors can see her teapot and her book of meditation. The staff will give you an engaging tour of the house. And if you are fortunate, you may even have an encounter with the spirits that call the Mary Washington House their home.

2

RISING SUN TAVERN

At 1304 Caroline Street stands the Rising Sun Tavern. On the front of the building is a large airy porch with benches that offer a welcoming place to sit. The history of the building known today at the Rising Sun Tavern is a fascinating window into the personalities and history of Fredericksburg in the eighteenth and nineteenth centuries. During the building's time as a tavern from 1792 to 1828, its name changed a few times. Period newspaper ads referred to the building as "under the Sign of the Rising Sun Tavern" and the Golden Eagle. To prevent confusion, I will refer to the building as the Golden Eagle only during the period that it was operated under that name. For the rest of the building's history, I will refer to it as the Rising Sun Tavern.

Charles Washington was born on May 2, 1738, at Little Hunting Creek, Virginia, to Augustine and Mary Ball Washington. Little Hunting Creek, the Washingtons' largest plantation, is now known as Mount Vernon. Charles did not reside at Little Hunting Creek for long, as shortly after his birth, he moved with his family to Ferry Farm in Stafford County, Virginia. Ferry Farm would be Charles's childhood home. At Ferry Farm, Charles lived with his parents and his older siblings George, Betty, Samuel and John Augustine. In 1739, Mildred joined the Washington family, but sadly she died from illness in 1740 at the age of sixteen months. The death of his baby sister would not be the only loss that Charles encountered during his childhood. In 1743, Augustine Washington died, leaving the five-year-old boy without a father.

Following Augustine Washington's death, Charles was raised by his mother at Ferry Farm. From his father's estate, Charles inherited enslaved people and a portion of seven hundred acres that was divided between himself and his older brothers Samuel and John Augustine. At the age of five, Charles Washington became an enslaver. Concerned about her children's future, Mary Washington ensured that her children, including Charles, received etiquette lessons required as part of the gentry class. Mary's hard work paid off, and in 1757, Charles married his cousin Mildred Thornton, a member of the wealthy Thornton family.

In 1759, as a member of the gentry, Charles Washington purchased 759 acres of land in the Berkeley District of Spotsylvania County. That same year, Mildred Washington gave birth to the couple's first child, a son they named George Augustine. Furthering his landholdings in 1761, Charles purchased two lots for £80 in Fredericksburg from Warner Lewis, the father of his brother-in-law, Fielding Lewis. On this lot, Charles constructed a home for his family; this building would become known as the Rising Sun Tavern. As a prominent citizen of Fredericksburg, Charles became a vestryman and a

The Rising Sun Tavern was built by Charles Washington as a home for his family in the early 1760s. Today, staff and guests report interacting with the ghost of tavern keeper John Frazer. *Author's photo.*

warden at St. George's Anglican (now Episcopal) Church. Charles was also a Mason and was a member of Freemason Lodge No. 4, which was the same lodge that George Washington joined in 1753.

The house at 1304 Caroline Street was completed in 1762, and Charles and Mildred Washington moved into their new townhouse. While living in Fredericksburg, George Washington visited his brother's home several times. George Washington became particularly fond of his nephew and namesake George Augustine Washington. In 1765, a second son, Samuel, joined the family at the Charles Street residence. Charles Washington became a magistrate of Spotsylvania County. In colonial Virginia, a magistrate was a justice of the peace who dealt with minor crimes. To support his family, Charles was involved in several business ventures, including owning a plantation in Spotsylvania County and a partnership in a meat butchering business with George Weedon. Charles also assisted his brother George in land speculation in the western territories; he bought tracts of land and then transferred the ownership to George, which allowed the elder Washington brother to amass large landholdings. Along with assisting his brother in business ventures, Charles also supported George in his political campaigns.

Charles Washington was also politically active in the 1760s. On February 27, 1766, Charles signed the Leedstown Resolution, a proposal written by Richard Henry Lee in protest of the Stamp Act. The Leedstown Resolution was the first public protest of the Stamp Act, which had been passed by Parliament in 1765. Other signers of the resolves were Richard Henry Lee, Thomas Ludwell Lee, Francis Lightfoot Lee and Francis Thornton Jr. Charles affixed his name to the resolves alongside his brothers Samuel Washington, Lawrence Washington and John Augustine Washington.

As tensions between the colonists and Great Britain increased, Charles Washington was appointed to the position of commissary for the Virginia Troops for Stafford County in 1772. Also in 1772, Charles was appointed a colonel in the local militia, which he had helped organize, and was designated the keeper of the magazine that was to be built at the Fredericksburg Manufactory. Construction started on the magazine in Fredericksburg, but it was never completed. The magazine was where the militia stored their arms, ammunition and black powder. To be appointed to such a prestigious position illustrated that Charles Washington was a respected member of the community. Charles also canvassed for the signing of the Continental Articles of Association. At his Fredericksburg home, Charles continued to support his growing family. In 1772, Mildred gave birth to the couple's first daughter, Frances Ann.

In 1774, Charles Washington became a member of the committee of correspondence for the County of Spotsylvania. During the early years of the American Revolution, committees of correspondence allowed the Patriots to share information and coordinate resistance to the British throughout the North American colonies. The Virginia Committee of Correspondence was founded in 1773 after the *Gaspee* affair in Rhode Island. Following the burning of a customs ship, the Virginia House of Burgesses became alarmed by the British government's plan to transport the perpetrators to England to stand trial. Concerned by what they considered a usurpation of British authority, the House of Burgesses formed a committee of correspondence to communicate with neighboring colonies. Local committees of correspondence were founded in 1774 to select a delegate for the First Continental Congress and to resist the Coercive Acts, which were passed by Parliament to punish Boston following the Boston Tea Party. After the start of the Revolutionary War in 1775, Charles was appointed to the Spotsylvania County Committee of Safety. In the political vacuum created by the Revolutionary War, committees of safety served as de facto local governments prior to the Declaration on Independence and the ratification of the Virginia state constitution. Charles Washington remained active in these organizations for the remainder of the 1770s.

During the war, Charles and Mildred welcomed their last child, a girl they named Mildred. After the birth of Mildred in 1779, Charles decided to sell his home in Fredericksburg and move his growing family to land that he had inherited from his half-brother Lawrence Washington in 1759. The 1,106-acre tract was located in Frederick County, Virginia (now Jefferson County, West Virginia), and was ideal for building a plantation. It is unclear why Charles decided to uproot his family in 1780, but the economic instability brought on by the Revolutionary War was likely a key factor in his decision. Charles decided to follow his older brother Samuel's example and settle in what was then western Virginia. Samuel had moved his family to Frederick County in 1772. The largely unsettled wilderness of Frederick County offered Charles the chance to rebuild his fortune and become a founding member and leading landowner of the county. It also helped that he would be supported by his brother as he established himself in Frederick County.

To pay for his move to Frederick County, Charles Washington sold off his seven-hundred-acre property in Spotsylvania County. Charles then gifted his home at 1304 Caroline Street to his oldest son, George Augustine Washington. In 1780, Charles moved his family to Frederick County and established a plantation that he named Happy Retreat. Charles's new home was located four miles away from Samuel's plantation, Harewood. Sadly, the brothers did not have much time to enjoy each other's company, as Samuel succumbed to tuberculosis in 1781. Charles established himself as a leading member of Frederick County, and in the mid-1780s, he laid out the plans for a town located near Happy Retreat. In 1786, the Virginia Assembly passed the act that formally created Charles Town, Virginia (now West Virginia), on eighty acres that were owned by Charles. While laying out the streets, Charles named several after members of his family.

Charles Washington lived at Happy Retreat for the remainder of his life. The final decade of Charles's life was difficult due to financial setbacks. By 1799, his health had started to deteriorate. In preparation for his death, Charles wrote his will on July 25, 1799. Two months later, Charles died from an unknown ailment on September 20, 1799, at the age of sixty-one. Following his death, he was buried at Happy Retreat, his beloved home. Upon hearing the news that his last surviving sibling had died, George wrote sadly, "I was the first, and am now the last, of my father's children by the second marriage who remain….When I shall be called upon to follow them is known only to the giver of life." George joined his siblings three months later, dying on December 14, 1799.

In 1780, when he was twenty-one years old, George Augustine Washington was given the title of the property at 1304 Caroline Street by his father, Charles Washington. George Augustine had lived at the house since his family had moved into the property in 1762, but he would never live in the house after his father gave him the property. In 1777, George Augustine followed in the footsteps of his illustrious uncle General George Washington and joined the military to fight for his country's independence. George Augustine first joined a light horse cavalry unit; the next year, he joined a partisan legion, where he was commissioned a cornet under the command of Major Henry Lee. But due to ill health, which would plague him for the remainder of his life, George Augustine resigned his commission by the end of 1778. Determined to still serve his county, in the summer of 1779, George Augustine volunteered as an aide-de-camp at General George Washington's headquarters. By February 1780, George Augustine Washington had recovered sufficiently to be commissioned an ensign in the Second Virginia Regiment and was detached for duty with General Washington's personal bodyguards called the "Life Guards."

During the Virginia campaign in the summer of 1781, George Augustine Washington was appointed the aide-de-camp to the Marquis de Lafayette. Though beset with illness, George Augustine served with distinction during the siege of Yorktown. Following the Marquis de Lafayette's return to France, George Augustine resumed his duties as part of his uncle's military family. But ill health again prevented him from serving as an aide for long, and George Augustine spent the next three years traveling to find relief from what had become tuberculosis. In May 1785, George Augustine returned to Virginia to live with George and Martha Washington at Mount Vernon, where he would remain for the remainder of his life. At Mount Vernon, George Augustine found love and married Martha Washington's favorite niece, Frances "Fanny" Bassett, on October 15, 1785. The couple would have four children.

Starting in 1786, George Augustine Washington served as the overseer of Mount Vernon supervising the management of the plantation during George Washington's frequent absences. During this period, George Augustine's health continued to deteriorate. On February 5, 1793, George Augustine Washington died at Eltham, the plantation of his wife's family. Six years later, George Washington remembered his beloved nephew when he left a bequest to George Augustine's three surviving children. "As on account of the affection I had for, and the obligation I was under to, their father when living, who from his youth had attached himself to my person, and followed my fortunes through the vicissitudes of the late Revolution—afterwards devoting his time to the Superintendence of my private concerns for many years…thereby affording me essential Services, and always performing them in manner the most filial and respectful," George Washington wrote in 1799.

George Augustine Washington never lived in the Rising Sun Tavern after he joined the Continental army. Instead of residing there, George Augustine used it as a rental property, renting it to friends and family members. Near the end of his life in 1792, George Augustine sold the property to Larkin Smith. Like its prior owner, Smith did not reside in the house but sold the property nine months later to Colonel Gustavus Brown Wallace. It was during the Wallace family's ownership that the house was turned into a tavern.

Gustavus Brown Wallace was born on November 9, 1751, in King George County, Virginia, to Dr. Michael Wallace and Elizabeth Brown. Gustavus Brown Wallace joined the Continental army in 1776. Wallace was commissioned a captain in the Third Virginia Regiment and was promoted to major of the regiment in 1777. During the winter of 1777–78, Wallace was at Valley Forge with General George Washington's army. After the fall of Charleston, South Carolina, in May 1780, Wallace became a prisoner of war until Governor Thomas Nelson was able to secure his release. In addition to the property that became known as the Rising Sun Tavern, Wallace owned a livery stable and was a breeder of greyhounds.

After purchasing the Rising Sun Tavern, Wallace put the property up for rent. One month after the purchase, Wallace found a tenant for the house. John Frazer leased the building and turned it into a tavern in May 1792 under "the Sign of the Golden Eagle." Frazer was also a veteran of the American Revolution. Before the war, Frazer had graduated from the College of William & Mary. One of the Rising Sun Tavern's prized items is the original tavern license dated March 1793 and signed by John Frazer. As noted, the tavern opened in September 1792, so there is a possibility that John Frazer was operating the Golden Eagle Tavern without a license for the first six months of its operation. Unlicensed taverns were not uncommon in the eighteenth century, and it was common for tavern keepers to let their tavern license expire before renewing it. The tavern license is also unique in that it was printed before the American Revolution: the wording on the document states that the authority to run a tavern in "the colony of Virginia" was granted by King George III. Instead of rewording and reprinting the document, city officials crossed out the out-of-date wording and wrote in that the license was granted to the commonwealth of Virginia under Governor Henry Lee.

The plans that John Frazer may have had for the Golden Eagle Tavern was dashed when he died suddenly in November 1793. Following John Frazer's death, his widow, Elizabeth Fox Frazer, remained as the tavern keeper of the Golden Eagle until 1795. In the eighteenth century, it was common for women to be tavern keepers. Taverns were family affairs, with a wife assisting her husband in the daily operations of the tavern. After the death of a male owner, it was common for the widow to continue to operate the tavern after her husband's death. During this period, being a tavern keeper was seen as a respectable occupation for a woman. Taverns in this period were more than just places where a person could get an alcoholic beverage. It is estimated that between 33 and 50 percent of taverns in America during this period were operated by women. Elizabeth Fox Frazer would not be the only woman to operate a tavern at 1304 Caroline Street.

While Elizabeth Fox Frazer managed the books and welcomed guests, the hard work of cleaning, caring for guests and cooking was performed by enslaved Black men, women and children. Throughout the site's time as the Golden Eagle Tavern, the number of enslaved workers on the property fluctuated between four and twelve people. Even children as young as twelve years old worked in the Golden Eagle Tavern, performing the necessary labor to keep the tavern in operation. Despite working in the kitchens, serving customers with food and drink, cleaning rooms, laundering linens, and stabling guests' horses, the enslaved workers did not reap the rewards of their labor. All profit that these men, women and children earned for the tavern went directly to Mistress Frazer.

In January 1795, an advertisement was placed in the *Virginia Herald* stating that the Eagle Tavern was for rent. The next operator of the Golden Eagle was James Fisher, who placed an advertisement in the *Virginia Herald* that the Golden Eagle was operating as an "House of Entertainment." In the Federal period, a house of entertainment was a place where drinks, music, performances and other forms of entertainment were provided. During this period, James Fisher took out a Mutual Fire Assurance Policy in which the property was described as consisting of one wood building covered with wood (in other words, wood siding) with a matching front and back porch, though the back porch was divided with a shed on either end where supplies were stored. A kitchen stood forty-two feet off the back right end of the building with a small meat house beside it. Finally, a billiards building had been constructed in the yard located left of center of the back porch. Sadly, none of these outbuildings have survived.

James Fisher operated a successful tavern until his death in 1798. Following his death, James Fisher's widow, Martha Fisher, became the next tavern keeper of the Golden Eagle. In July 1801, Colonel Wallace transferred ownership of 1304 Caroline Street to his sons John and Thomas Wallace. Colonel Wallace may have given his sons the property because he was preparing for a long visit to Scotland. Tragedy struck the Wallace family in August 1802 when Colonel Wallace died from typhus upon his return from Scotland. The next month, Martha Fisher advertised in the *Virginia Herald* that she was moving her tavern to the location of General George Weedon's tavern. This move was likely because there was a ownership dispute following Colonel Wallace's death.

In the fall of 1803, the Wallace brothers tried to sell the property but were unable to find a buyer. The brothers tried to sell the site in 1805 and were again unsuccessful. Unable to find a buyer or a tenant, the building was listed as unoccupied in town records. In the fire of 1807, which destroyed twenty-six houses and many stores and warehouses—including Mistress Fisher's tavern—the Rising Sun Tavern site was spared. After the fire, Martha Fisher moved the Golden Eagle Tavern back to 1304 Caroline Street. The tavern continued to be successful for the rest of the decade, but by 1810, Martha had started to experience financial difficulties. Martha continued to operate the Golden Eagle Tavern until 1812, when she disappeared from the historical record.

The next occupant was John Harvey, who moved into the building in 1813. In 1815, the Wallace brothers tried to sell the building, listing that the property would be sold at auction. The Mutual Fire Assurance Policy from this time gives us a glimpse of how the property looked. Along with a one-story building with matching front and back porches, there was listed a "Dwelling house 1½ story all wood" placed seven feet to the right of the main house. The house was not sold at auction, and Richard Tutt became the next person to rent the house.

Like the previous occupants, Richard Tutt operated a tavern and place of entertainment at the site. Tutt hosted a slackwire exhibition and other forms of entertainment at the site. In November 1817, Tutt proclaimed in an advertisement that the building had "undergone considerable repair.... He can accommodate the weary Travellers [*sic*] with as comfortable beds and as good accommodations in every other respect as any tavern in this place." It appears the tavern was not successful, and the Wallace brothers tried to sell the building again in 1818. Richard Tutt was the last person to operate a tavern at the site.

In 1819, John Wallace bought his share of the property from his brother Thomas. Now as the sole owner of 1304 Caroline Street, John Wallace placed the building up for rent but was unable to find a tenant until 1821. Finally, Wallace found M. Verone, who lived in the Rising Sun Tavern building until his death in 1829. The building ceased operating as a tavern in 1828, when the tavern license was revoked for unknown reasons. Following Verone's death, the site remained vacant until 1843. John Wallace owned the building until his death in 1851. The site would pass through the Wallace family for the remainder of the nineteenth century.

During the Civil War, the building was hit by cannon fire and used as a hospital. One of the legends connected with the building claims that the original floorboards were ruined from the bloodstains from the wounded soldiers. In 1907, the Association for the Preservation of Virginia Antiquities (APVA) purchased the house. The APVA restored the building and opened it as a museum under the name of the Rising Sun Tavern in 1910. The building was restored in the 1930s, and the porch was rebuilt in the 1970s. The Rising Sun Tavern became part of the Washington Heritage Museums in 2012. Today the Rising Sun Tavern educates visitors from around the world about the Washington family and tavern life during the Federal era.

With such a rich history, it is no surprise that the Rising Sun Tavern has acquired a reputation for being haunted. The paranormal activity at the Rising Sun Tavern fits the building's nature. While the ghosts that haunt the Mary Washington House are genteel in nature and let their presence be known in subtle ways, the ghosts of the Rising Sun Tavern act out in a rollicking, boisterous nature, fitting for the site of a former tavern. The activity at the site is mischievous and generally harmless, though the biggest complaint is that the ghosts of the Rising Sun Tavern do not have modern sensibilities when it comes to personal space.

John Frazer is blamed for most of the paranormal activity at the Rising Sun Tavern. Frazer died suddenly of an unknown ailment in November 1793. According to legend, Frazer was stricken at the tavern and became so ill that he could not be taken to his home and died in an upstairs bedroom. It is alleged that Frazer died in the second-best bedroom, located on the left-hand side of the tavern's second floor. Because Frazer's death was so unexpected and he had only just opened his tavern, it is believed that his rollicking spirit chose to stay in the building. Paranormal activity at the Rising Sun Tavern is the most active in November, around the anniversary of Frazer's death. A popular yearly event at the Rising Sun Tavern is held in November to commemorate Frazer's death and the ghost stories about the site.

The bedroom where it is believed John Frazer died in is known for having odd things occur in it. Once, a guide was frustrated that she had to repeatedly enter the room after something, or someone, kept unplugging the lights. The guide had to unlatch the barricade and plug the light back into the socket. Aggravated, she scolded the ghost. "Come on now, stop it!" she exclaimed. The ghost did not appreciate being scolded, and as the guide was leaving the room, the rug was pulled out from under her, causing her to fall. Fortunately, she was not injured. Other strange activity around this room includes the sound of a man in heavy boots walking on the hardwood floors.

I have witnessed strange activity in this bedroom. During an investigation conducted by Culpeper Paranormal Investigations, a group of paranormal investigators from Culpeper County, Virginia, I witnessed their equipment interacting with something. The group had set up a device that lit up when it movement on the floor near the fireplace. We made sure that we were far enough away from the equipment so that we would not accidentally interact with it. While the group was focusing on reviewing an EVP session, I happened to notice that the lights of the device were slowly lighting up. We then started to ask whoever was influencing the device to light it up, resulting in an interaction with someone or something that seemed to be intelligent. Our conversation with the entity was interrupted when we heard a loud bang coming from the tavern's best bedroom, which was down the hall. Not wanting to miss any potential evidence, we all went down the hall to see what was going on in that room. We could find nothing amiss in that room. While we were familiarizing ourselves with the best bedroom, we all heard something being kicked, and the sound came from the direction of the room we had just exited. It felt like someone was playing a game with us.

Guides have reported coming into the Rising Sun Tavern in the morning and finding postcards or tricornered hats knocked to the ground. Once two guides witnessed playing cards on display on a table in the tavern room get knocked off the table and go flying across the room. That was too much for them, and they closed the museum early.

Female staff have reported having their caps pulled off their heads. Once while going down the stairs, a guide was stopped when she felt someone pulling on the back of her petticoat. The tugging lasted only a moment, and she was able to continue her journey. What is intriguing about this story is that her co-workers witnessed the back of her petticoat pulled out, like someone had it in their hand. This is not the only time that something like this has occurred. A guide who worked at the Hugh Mercer Apothecary Shop who also conducted ghost tours in the evening told me about the time she was standing on the porch of the tavern during a tour. She was telling her group about John Frazer when she felt the back of her petticoat being touched. She said it felt like someone had grabbed the back and was lifting it up by the hem. At first, she thought that she had gotten her petticoat caught on something and she took a step forward while she continued to talk. But she still felt like someone was playing with the back of her hem. By this point, someone in her tour group cried out that they were seeing the back of her petticoat moving by unseen hands. Creeped out by what was going on, she decided to cut her presentation short and move on to the next stop on her tour route.

The ghosts also like to play pranks on the staff during the day. One afternoon, two guides were sitting in the entryway, as it was a quiet day. Suddenly, they both heard glass breaking in the taproom. The guides rushed into the room expecting to see smashed glass everywhere, but they were shocked to find the room intact. Puzzled, they returned to the entryway. A few minutes later, they both heard glass clinking in the parlor. To them it sounded like a person was putting a tray laden with glasses on a table. Whoever was bustling about in the parlor, the spectral waiter remained unseen.

Another spirit was identified several years ago by paranormal researchers. During an investigation in 2017, members of the Culpeper Paranormal Investigations were investigating the Rising Sun Tavern. When reviewing an EVP session, the group could clearly hear an answer to one of their questions. "Can you please tell us your name?" team member Jayne Ramirez asked. On the recorder, a woman answered, "Elizabeth." Elizabeth Frazer was John Frazer's wife, and following her husband's death in 1792, she served as tavern keeper until 1795. Is the spirit of Elizabeth still looking after her rowdy husband?

The strangest account I have heard occurred at the Rising Sun Tavern happened on March 17, 2012, to paranormal author and investigator Mark Nesbitt. Known in the paranormal community as the author of *The Ghosts of Gettysburg* series, Mark had come to Fredericksburg with his group to conduct investigations at several haunted locations. While in the cellar, Mark heard a strange "whooshing" sound like something that had a "canned" sound from an old movie. According to Mark:

> Immediately after that there was male laughter—not sinister, but, once again sounding "canned." At first I thought it was coming from my recorder, then from the door, then from the air ducts. The whole thing lasted three or four seconds. I thought about pulling out my recorder, but thought, because the sound was so canned and realistic, that it was probably someone from the Tavern playing a prank, a recording through the ductwork.

At the conclusion of the investigation, Mark questioned the manager of the tavern about the prank that he believed had been pulled on him. The manager was confused and told Mark that no one beside her knew that a group would be at the tavern that night, and she was not the sort of person to pull foolish pranks on people.

I highly recommend a visit to the Rising Sun Tavern to learn about the life of Charles Washington and about what it was like to visit a tavern in the Federal period. The history of the site features many complex and colorful characters that brings history to life, and if you are lucky, you might get to encounter the mischievous spirit of John Frazer, who is still walking the halls of his tavern more than two hundred years after his death.

3

HUGH MERCER APOTHECARY SHOP

The Hugh Mercer Apothecary Shop, located at 1020 Caroline Street in downtown Fredericksburg, re-creates the sights and smells of an eighteenth-century apothecary shop. In the colonial area, apothecaries were where people could acquire needed medicines to cure ailments or injuries. Frequently run by doctors, apothecaries acted like what we would call a pharmacy or a drugstore today. Medical operations were rarely done in an apothecary shop, as physicians in this period conducted house calls to treat the sick in their own homes. The Hugh Mercer Apothecary Shop not only serves as a medical museum but also tells the story of the life of Dr. Hugh Mercer, who was a prominent doctor in Fredericksburg and a general in the Continental army who gave his life for his adopted country.

Like the Rising Sun Tavern, the story of the building known as the Hugh Mercer Apothecary Shop is far richer and more complex than what appears on the surface. Despite being an eighteenth-century building, the site was never owned or used by Hugh Mercer during his time in Fredericksburg. It was originally misidentified as the site of the Hugh Mercer Apothecary Shop in the early twentieth century due to the building's age and because it was located near the area Hugh Mercer had his doctor's office and residence. In the eighteenth century, houses and shops did not have address numbers, making the location descriptions mentioned in colonial ads difficult to pinpoint with complete accuracy two hundred years later. Based on two advertisements that Hugh Mercer published in the *Virginia Gazette*, the actual location of his apothecary shop was likely on modern-day Amelia Street facing Caroline Street. It is believed that Hugh Mercer's apothecary shop was destroyed in the Fredericksburg fire of 1807. Regardless, the site of the Hugh Mercer Apothecary Shop has a rich history that illustrates the plight of those who chose to remain Loyalists during the American Revolution. But before I discuss the history of 1020 Caroline Street, it's important to cover the life of Dr. Hugh Mercer.

Hugh Mercer was born on January 16, 1726, in Pitsligo, Aberdeenshire, Scotland, to William and Ann Monro Mercer. William Mercer was a minister in the Church of Scotland; this allowed his son to receive an excellent education. Mercer studied medicine at Marischal College in Aberdeen, Scotland from 1740 to 1744. In the eighteenth century, most doctors received their medical education by apprenticing to a physician who would pass on his knowledge to his apprentice. Dr. Mercer graduated in time to become involved in the Jacobite rising of 1745. It is unclear why Mercer joined the forces of Charles Stuart (Bonnie Prince Charlie) in the attempt to reclaim the British throne for his father, James Francis Edward Stuart. Whether for loyalty to the House of Stuart, a dislike for the Hanoverians, an

The Hugh Mercer Apothecary Shop was built by merchant Henry Mitchell, who was forced to sell the building after being banished from Virginia during the Revolutionary War for being a Loyalist. *Author's photo*.

opposition to the 1707 Union or from Scottish nationalism, Mercer served as a surgeon's mate with the Jacobite rebels. After the Jacobite defeat at the Battle of Culloden in April 1746, Mercer went into hiding to escape British retribution. In the fall of 1746, Mercer sailed from Leith, Scotland, to Philadelphia, Pennsylvania.

Mercer settled on the Pennsylvania frontier in 1750 near Greencastle, now modern-day Mercersburg, and set up a medical practice and apothecary. With the start of the French and Indian War in 1755, Mercer joined the Pennsylvania militia. Mercer's first major engagement in the war was as part of General Edward Braddock's failed attempt to capture Fort Duquesne. The expedition was a failure, and Mercer was wounded in the arm. The wound was minor, and by March 1756, Mercer had been commissioned a captain in a Pennsylvania regiment and was given the command of Fort Shirley. In September 1756, Captain Mercer participated in the Kittanning Expedition under the command of Lieutenant Colonel John Armstrong. During the engagement at Kittanning, Mercer was seriously wounded and separated from his unit. Alone and injured, Mercer trekked one hundred miles through hostile territory for fourteen days. Mercer was rescued by a company of Cherokee who were assisting the British. They carried Mercer to Fort Lyttleton, where he was able to receive medical attention. The next year, Mercer was promoted to major and was given command of the garrison at Shippensburg. By 1758, Mercer had been promoted to lieutenant colonel and was tasked with joining the Forbes Expedition to capture the French-held Fort Duquesne. It was during this time that Mercer met Colonel George Washington. After the successful capture of Fort Duquesne, Mercer was tasked with command of the fort for nine months until construction on the new Fort Pitt began. During the French and Indian War, Mercer gained recognition for his professionalism.

Following the war, Mercer moved to Fredericksburg, Virginia, where he would establish a successful medical practice. In Fredericksburg, Mercer met his wife, Isabella Gordon. With Isabella, Mercer had five children: William Mercer (born 1765), George Mercer (1767), Ann Gorden Mercer Patton (1770), John Mercer (1771) and Hugh Tennant Weedon Mercer (1776). Two of Hugh's sons were deaf. Mercer was a popular and a well-respected member of the community and befriended another Scottish expatriate, the merchant John Paul Johns. In 1761, Mercer joined Masonic Lodge No. 4. Known for his convivial manner, Mercer was frequently found at his brother-in-law's tavern. George Weedon's tavern was the central gathering place for those sympathetic to the Patriot cause. Along with maintaining a successful medical practice, Mercer also became a property owner in 1764 when he won three lots in a lottery. In 1766, Mercer purchased a home for his growing family when he bought Lot 50 on Amelia Street for £480 from James Hunter—an expensive purchase at the time. Mercer also owned enslaved workers who would have cared for his family and may have assisted Mercer in his apothecary.

As a testament to his successful practice in Fredericksburg, Hugh Mercer was able to take Dr. Ewen Clement as a partner in 1771. The partnership financially benefited Mercer, as he received two-thirds of the income collected from their clients. The next year, in 1772, Mercer accepted John Julian, son of a local tavern keeper, as his new partner. During this period, Mercer's practice flourished; between 1771 to 1773, Mercer recorded having over one hundred patients.

Mercer's patients included members of the gentry, successful merchants, craftsmen and tavern keepers. He also treated members of the Washington and Lewis family, including Mary Washington and her enslaved workers at Ferry Farm. While Mary Washington was ill with influenza in the winter of 1771–72, Mercer frequently made house calls at Ferry Farm. After Mary Washington moved to Fredericksburg, George Washington placed Ferry Farm up for sale. Initially, Washington was unable to find a buyer for the plantation, but in 1774, Hugh Mercer was financially secure enough to purchase the property. In a letter to George Washington, Mercer wrote: "Ever since I understood that the Land whereon Mrs. Washington lived [was] for Sale I have had an Inclination to purchase it, but till now was not in circumstances to propose the matter to you." Mercer initially offered £1,800 for the property but in the end accepted Washington's counteroffer of £2,000 in five annual payments. Mercer dreamed of turning the property into a town where he would raise his family for the rest of his life. Because of the Revolutionary War, Mercer never lived on the property. Following Mercer's death, the property passed to Mercer's children, who sold Ferry Farm to John Coalter in 1829.

In 1775, Hugh Mercer rented the location of John Jones's ordinary (tavern) as the site of his medical office and apothecary. Mercer would have rarely treated patients at his rented office. In the eighteenth century, doctors made house calls; they treated patients and even conducted operations in the home of the patient. For a home visit, Mercer charged his patients five shillings. At his apothecary, Mercer dispensed medication that he had procured and made for his patients.

An ardent Patriot, Mercer was an active member of the Spotsylvania Committee of Safety. In 1775, Mercer was named the head of the Spotsylvania Independent Company of Horse. Following Patrick Henry's "Give me Liberty, or give me Death" speech delivered at St. John's Episcopal Church in Richmond in March 1775, royal governor Lord Dunmore, fearing an armed insurrection, ordered that the colony's supply of gunpowder kept at the magazine in Williamsburg be removed. In the dead of night on April 20, 1775, the gunpowder was removed and taken to the safety of a British warship moored in the James River. When word of the Gunpowder Incident reached Fredericksburg a few days later, Mercer sent word to the militias in the adjoining counties to assemble in Fredericksburg to march on Williamsburg to demand the return of the colony's gunpowder. Mercer dispatched a message to George Washington at Mount Vernon detailing the proposed march. Fortunately, cooler heads prevailed, and the march on Williamsburg was canceled.

Mercer was also appointed a colonel of the local minutemen in September 1775. Despite having no military experience, Patrick Henry was appointed as the head of the First Virginia Regiment. Mercer was passed over in favor of Henry because Mercer was Scottish or, as it was labeled, a "northern Briton." Regardless of this snub, Mercer was elected the colonel of the Minute Men of Spotsylvania, King George, Stafford and Caroline Counties. Mercer was appointed an officer in the Second Virginia Regiment, and on December 12, 1775, he was appointed as the colonel of the Third Virginia Regiment. Under Mercer in the Third Virginia Regiment was future president James Monroe and future chief justice of the United States John Marshall.

In February 1776, the Continental Congress took six of the nine Virginia regiments into the Continental army. Before leaving Fredericksburg, Mercer wrote his will. In his will, Mercer detailed his considerable landholdings, which included three lots in Fredericksburg, three hundred acres at Fall Hill, Ferry Farm and western lands that he had purchased from George Weedon and James Duncanson. Mercer wanted to make sure that his wife and children were provided for if he should die during the war. After settling his affairs, Hugh Mercer and George Weedon traveled to Williamsburg to accept their commissions in the Continental army.

In June 1776, on the recommendation of General George Washington, Hugh Mercer was appointed a brigadier general in the Continental army. General Mercer joined the Continental army in New Jersey. Upon his arrival in New Jersey, Mercer was given the command of the Flying Corps, a mobile corps of militia that was stationed on the central New Jersey shore that was used as a screen against the British forces stationed at Staten Island. While in New Jersey, news arrived that his wife, Isabella, had given birth to a son on August 4, 1776. Hugh Mercer never got a chance to meet his youngest son, Hugh Tennant Weedon Mercer. By the fall of 1776, Mercer's Flying Corps had been depleted by desertion and the expiration of the term of service of his militiamen. A brigade was cobbled together for General Mercer before the Battle of Trenton. On December 25, 1776, Mercer crossed the Delaware with Washington's army and was part of the sneak attack on Trenton the next morning. Following the victory at Trenton, the Continental army attacked British general Lord Cornwallis's army at Princeton, New Jersey, on January 3, 1777.

General Mercer led the first troops into the battle. With a contingent of 350 men, Mercer's forces engaged in combat with a force of 700 British troops under the command of Lieutenant Colonel Charles Mawhood. Vastly outnumbered, Mercer's troops put up a valiant stand in William Clarke's orchard. After an exchange of musket fire, the British troops bayonet charged Mercer's forces. Mercer ordered a retreat, and in the mêlée, he was unhorsed when his horse was shot out from under him. Immediately surrounded by the British, Mercer drew his sword and prepared to fight to the death. Ordered to surrender, Mercer refused and was clubbed over the head and bayoneted seven times. According to legend, one of the reasons that Mercer was so viciously attacked was because some of the British soldiers believed that they had cornered General George Washington. In agony, Mercer was dragged from the battlefield and placed under a white oak tree where he watched the remainder of the battle. General Washington saved his army by entering the battle and rallying Mercer's troops, pushing the British troops from the field.

Following the battle, General Mercer was brought to the Thomas Clarke House, where he was placed in a spare bedroom. Despite his grievous wounds, which included a bayonet that was still impaled in his body, Mercer was in good spirits. "Cheer up my boys, the day is ours," he exclaimed. Though the battle had been successful, Washington's forces withdrew from Princeton, leaving Mercer behind. Under a flag of truce, Washington sent his nephew Captain George Washington Lewis to care for his wounded friend. Captain Lewis knew Mercer, as the physician had cared for him and his family in Fredericksburg. Dr. Benjamin Rush from Philadelphia was also summoned to care for Mercer. Despite the best efforts of Dr. Rush and Captain Lewis, Mercer died in Lewis's arms on January 12, 1777. After his death, Mercer's body was transported to Philadelphia, where a public viewing was held at City Tavern. Following his military funeral, Mercer was buried in Christ Church Graveyard, where he remained until 1840, when his remains were moved to Philadelphia's Laurel Hill Cemetery. Mercer's death was mourned by his brothers in arms, including General George Washington, who declared in his report to Congress, "[The victory at Princeton] was counterbalanced by the loss of the brave and worthy General Mercer."

Following her husband's death, Isabella Gordon Mercer had the responsibility of caring for her five children. To support them, Isabella continued to lease her husband's office space at the Jones tavern. She continued to live at her home on Amelia Street with her daughter until her death in 1791. General George Weedon, who had married Isabella's sister, Catherine Gordon Weedon, helped his sister-in-law care for her children. George and Catherine Weedon were childless and became the legal guardians of the Mercer children. Weedon was able to send William Mercer to Philadelphia to receive artistic training under Charles Wilson Peale. William Mercer, who was deaf, became America's first deaf artist. In a letter written to Peale in 1786, Weedon wrote about William: "I am sure it will give you pleasure to hear from your pupil Will'm Mercer. I wrote you some time since that I was likely to succeed with his female friends in sending him back to you for six months more. It [h]as been a trying task, however, they have at last consented to part with him again." Following General Weedon's death in 1793, his nephew Hugh Tennant Weedon Mercer inherited his Fredericksburg residence known as the Sentry Box.

General Hugh Mercer's direct decedents include such luminaries as General George S. Patton Jr., Confederate general Hugh Weedon Mercer and songwriter Johnny Mercer. Mercer's legacy also lives on in pop culture: in the 2000 TV movie *The Crossing*, General Hugh Mercer is played by actor Roger Rees. The movie focuses on the crossing of the Delaware and the Battle of Trenton. Mercer is also mentioned in the song "The Room Where It Happens" written by Lin-Manuel Miranda for *Hamilton: An American Musical*. In the song, Aaron Burr and Alexander Hamilton discuss the news that a street in Manhattan has been renamed in Mercer's honor.

The building that is now known as the Hugh Mercer Apothecary Shop was built between 1771 and 1772 and was the location of Henry Mitchell's store. Henry Mitchell was born in Scotland and arrived in Fredericksburg in 1757. During the colonial era, Fredericksburg was a bustling and vibrant community. Located on the Rappahannock River, which fed into the

Chesapeake Bay, Fredericksburg was a port of call of merchant ships from around the world. Because of its size and location, Fredericksburg was the county seat for Spotsylvania County, and landowners were required by law to have their tobacco crop inspected and shipped to London from the city. Tobacco counting houses and warehouses lined the streets near the docks where tobacco was sold for hard currency, while on Caroline Street, residents and visitors could find shops and taverns to spend their profits. If a person did not have hard currency, they could pay for goods and services with tobacco.

Henry Mitchell came to Fredericksburg to earn his living as a merchant. He had been a part of the community and by the 1770s was well respected. Mitchell was a frequent visitor to George Weedon's tavern, where he drank and mingled with Dr. Hugh Mercer and Mann Page Jr. Before the war, Mitchell served as a factor for the firm of McCall Smellie and Co. and then as a partner with George McCall and Co.; both trading companies were based in Scotland. During the mid-eighteenth century, Fredericksburg and the surrounding counties had a large population of Scottish immigrants.

Following the Stamp Act in 1765, political relations with Great Britian began to sour in Virginia. After royal governor Norborne Berkeley, Lord Botetourt, dissolved the Virginia Assembly in 1769, the burgesses passed an agreement to boycott all British goods and imports. The association was signed on May 18, 1769, and copies of the agreement were sent home with the burgesses throughout Virginia. Initially, it appears that Henry Mitchell supported the association, as he was made an associator for Spotsylvania County on October 23, 1770. Mitchell joined alongside Fielding Lewis, Roger Dixon and Lewis Willis. The fact that Mitchell was selected illustrates that at this time he was well regarded by his neighbors.

Amid ongoing political turmoil of the early 1770s, Mitchell continued his business pursuits, which included serving as a trade partner with McCall, Smellie and Co. and purchasing property in Fredericksburg. In March 1771, Mitchell purchased the lot that would become 1020 Caroline Street from William and Mary Willis Daingerfield for £187. The property first appeared in records in 1740 when Henry Willis sold the property to his son John Willis. After 1749, Henry Lewis owned the property until his death, when it was passed to his niece Mary Willis Daingerfield. After purchasing the property, Mitchell had the structure that is now known as the Hugh Mercer Apothecary Shop built sometime between 1771 and 1772. Mitchell used the building as a store and published ads in the *Virginia Gazette* to inform the public about his wares. Coincidentally, one of his customers at the store at 1020 Caroline Street was Dr. Hugh Mercer, who recorded making purchases from Mitchell's store in his ledger in 1772.

Though initially sympathetic to the plight of the colonists, Mitchell considered himself a British citizen and remained loyal to England during the American Revolution. This decision would cost him dearly. The First Continental Congress held in the fall of 1774 signaled the start of the American Revolution. Though the colonists were still looking for a peaceful resolution with Great Britain, it was becoming clear that the divide between England and its colonies was deepening. On the local level, committees of correspondence and committees of safety were closely monitoring the personal loyalties of the populace. Those who professed loyalty to the Crown were publicly called out for condemnation.

In March 1775, Henry Mitchell came to the attention of the Committee of Safety of Orange County, Virginia, for owning political pamphlets. The pamphlets were in the possession of Reverand John Wingate, who had been reported to the committee of safety for having "several pamphlets, containing very obnoxious reflections on the Continental Congress." Wingate was ordered to turn the pamphlets over to the committee of safety so that they could be examined. Initially, Wingate refused because he claimed that the pamphlets belonged to Henry Mitchell and that he could not turn the pamphlets over without Mitchell's permission. This revelation shocked the committee of safety because Mitchell

> *was well known to be an associator, and acknowledged by himself to be a hearty friend to the cause which these pamphlets were intended to disparage and counteract; and that, if Mr. Mitchell was not this hearty friend we hoped him to be, it must be an additional argument, for the committee to pass their request, and for him to comply with it.*

Despite Wingate's protestations, the pamphlets belonging to Mitchell were seized and examined. The committee of safety decided that the pamphlets needed to be destroyed. On March 27, 1775, Mitchell's pamphlets were publicly burned. To ensure that everyone was aware of Mitchell's perceived duplicity, the Committee of Safety of Orange County submitted a lengthy account in the *Virginia Gazette*. Now that he was identified as a Loyalist, Mitchell's reputation and standing in Fredericksburg were damaged. In December 1775, Mitchell published a notice that he intended to leave the colony.

Despite professing an intention to leave, Mitchell was still in Fredericksburg in the summer of 1776, when he was called to appear before a local committee of Patriots to take an oath of loyalty to the Virginia Convention. Mitchell refused to take the oath and had his firearms taken away. In December 1776, Governor Patrick Henry ordered the expulsion of British immigrants, except those "such as them as have heretofore uniformly manifested a friendly disposition to the American cause, or are attached to this country by having wives and children here." Because Mitchell had refused to take the oath of loyalty and because he did not have a family to support, he was called to court on January 16, 1777. Mitchell appeared in the dock with eight other Loyalists and after "having nothing to offer in their defence [sic]" was ordered to be transmitted to appear before the governor in Williamsburg. Though ordered to leave Virginia, Mitchell was allowed to try to settle his affairs in Fredericksburg. In an advertisement placed in the *Virginia Gazette*, Mitchell expressed his intention to sell or rent his property in town. "The HOUSES and LOTS in Possession of *Henry Mitchell*, on the main Street in *Fredericksburg*, are to be sold or rented. The Houses are almost new, and very convenient for people in Trade," Mitchell wrote.

Mitchell left Fredericksburg in 1777 and was able to receive passage on the HMS *Phoenix* to the Loyalist stronghold of New York City. While in New York, Mitchell tried to support himself in trade. Following the British evacuation of New York City at the end of the Revolutionary War in 1781, Mitchell returned to his native Scotland to rebuild his life. Upon his arrival in Scotland, Mitchell discovered that the funds he had sent to his business partners during the Revolutionary War had been misapplied and that he was bankrupt. After decades of hard work, Mitchell had to be supported by family members. In desperation, Mitchell sold his store in Fredericksburg to Robert Johnston in 1782. Unable to support himself in Scotland, Mitchell returned to Fredericksburg in 1785. Mitchell remained in Virginia for the remainder of life, dying in Fredericksburg in the winter of 1793.

In 1786, Robert Johnston sold the property at 1020 Caroline Street to merchants David Henderson and Elieizer Callender. The site was used as a store. Following Callender's death in 1797, David Henderson purchased the property from Callender's estate. David Henderson ran a store and may have also lived in the building with his wife, Mildred, and his children. Henderson owned the property until 1843, when he sold the property to Hugh Patton, who was Hugh Mercer's grandson, to "secure payment for debt." Patton then sold the property to Mary Nelson and Elizabeth Henderson for $1,700.

Mary Nelson and Elizabeth Henderson owned the property until 1863, when they sold it to George Fitzhugh for $4,100. The building survived the Civil War because the structure is only one and a half stories. During the shelling of Fredericksburg in December 1862, artillery fire passed over the building, leaving it untouched.

During the 1920s, the building became a Ford dealership run by the Tompkins Motor Co. The Apothecary Room was used as the dealership room. In 1927, the building was purchased by the Citizen's Guild of Washington's Boyhood Home from its last private owner, John Gouldman. The building was restored and opened in 1928 as the Hugh Mercer Apothecary Shop by the Friends of Historic Pharmacy. Stewardship of the property passed to the Association for the Preservation of Virginia Antiquities, which became Preservation Virginia. In 2012, the Washington Heritage Museums was founded and now maintains the site. Today the Hugh Mercer Apothecary Shop educates the public on eighteenth-century medical treatments. Guests tour the Apothecary Room full of period pills and herbal remedies used to treat everything from cuts to heartburn. In the Doctor's Office Room, patrons learn about eighteenth-century surgery and can see live leeches on display. In the eighteenth century, leeches were used to bleed patients who were sick or injured. Along with the medical displays, visitors learn about the life of Hugh Mercer.

The past can still be felt at the Hugh Mercer Apothecary Shop. Though it is not as actively haunted as other sites in Fredericksburg, strange things have been reported by staff. Stories are told by the staff of hearing strange sounds in the building in the early hours of the morning. One morning, a guide had just arrived and was still in the back office putting his things away when he heard a loud crash coming from the Apothecary Room. The guide hurried down the small hallway past the display room, went through the Doctor's Office and was in the Apothecary Room in seconds. He expected to see the stool used by staff on the ground, but when he came into the room, the guide was shocked to find that everything was in its place. Another staff member reported that they heard a woman crying in the building. A guide saw a child's foot going up the stairs. All she saw was the single bare foot of a small child. Could this have been one of David and Mildred Henderson's children?

Could the angry spirit of Henry Mitchell be behind some of the activity at the Rising Sun Tavern? That is one possibility, as Mitchell lost his fortune and his standing in the community because of the American Revolution and now the building that he had built and lost is celebrating the life of a Patriot general while his achievements and suffering have been forgotten. During a living history event at the Apothecary Shop, a woman was in an upstairs bedroom knitting when suddenly one of the knitting needles was snatched from her hand and thrown across the room. Was this the disgruntled spirit of Henry Mitchell? I highly recommend that you visit the Hugh Mercer Apothecary Shop to learn about Dr. Hugh Mercer, who lost his life for his country, and marvel at how far medical treatment has changed in just two hundred years. But before you leave, remember Henry Mitchell, who lost his fortune for his country.

4

ST. GEORGE'S EPISCOPAL CHURCH

A t 905 Princess Anne Street stands St. George's Episcopal Church, the religious heart of Fredericksburg since 1720. The current church structure dates to 1849 and is an architectural gem. St. George's Parish was founded in 1720 to serve the spiritual needs of the English colonists. The Church of England (Anglican Church) was the state religion of England and its colonies. Along with serving the spiritual needs of the community, the Anglican Church also served as an arm of the British government by ensuring religious conformity in Virginia. St. George's Parish is older than the city of Fredericksburg, and a church building has been on the property since 1734. The property has seen the founding of a nation and a bloody civil war and has been at the center of struggles for equality. Many souls have passed through the property, and many remain permanently in the cemetery. But if the stories are true, not all the souls connected to St. George's rest peacefully.

The first church, known as the Rappahannock Church, was built ten miles west of Fredericksburg. With the official establishment of the city of Fredericksburg in 1728, the location of the Rappahannock Church quickly proved unsatisfactory, as residents had to travel a considerable distance to attend church. In the colonial period, residents were required by law to attend their parish church at least once a month. Failure to attend could result in a fine, imprisonment or banishment from the colony. In 1734, the second Rappahannock Church was constructed on the property that would become 905 Princess Anne Street. Next to the church building is the cemetery, which has been at that site since 1728; it is the oldest burial ground in the region. The church was constructed of wood, and it was this building where the Washington family worshiped. George Washington and his siblings may have attended the school run by the Reverend James Marye. The Parson's School opened in 1735 and provided a basic education to the children of Fredericksburg. In 1765, the Reverend Marye and Fielding Lewis opened a Bray School to educate enslaved and free Black children. The purpose of Bray Schools was to teach enslaved Black children to read the Bible and offer religious instruction in the tenets of the Anglican Church. It was believed that reading the Bible would make enslaved children more content with their lot as enslaved people. The Fredericksburg Bray School proved controversial with local enslavers, and the school closed in 1770 due to low attendance.

After the American Revolution and the passage of the Virginia Bill of Religious Freedom, Virginians could worship wherever they saw fit and

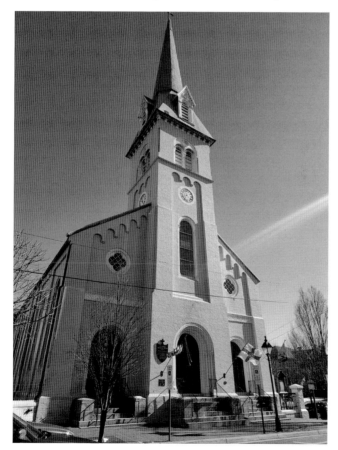

The first ghost sighting at St. George's Episcopal Church occurred in 1858, when a ghostly woman in white was seen praying at the altar. *Author's photo.*

many residents began attending the Baptist, Methodist or Presbyterian churches. In 1789, the church was renamed the Protestant Episcopal Church. Attendance was so low at this time that in 1813 the church vestry recorded only twelve members. In 1813, the Reverend Edward McGuire became the new rector, and under his tenure, he increased church membership. By the early nineteenth century, the original wood church had begun to deteriorate, and a new brick church was built in 1815. This church proved to be too small, and a new church was built in 1849. The current church was built in the Romanesque Revival style and is an elegant building. It was at this time that the church was renamed to St. George's Episcopal Church.

Before the Civil War, 251 congregants worshiped at St. George's. Beside regular services, the church also offered five Sunday schools, two of which were for enslaved people. The wealth of the church came from the labor of enslaved Black men, women and children. Reverend McGuire relied on the labor of his enslaved workers who cared for his home and children, allowing him to focus his efforts on his parishioners. Along with receiving a salary from the church, Reverend McGuire earned additional income by renting out the labor of his enslaved workers. While McGuire profited from slavery, he also supported the American Colonization Society (ACS), which advocated for the immigration of Black people to Liberia. Members of the ACS hoped that through settlement in Liberia, slavery in the United States would eventually be eradicated. The colonization movement failed due to difficulties finding Black colonists willing to leave their homes to settle in a foreign country and from the high mortality rate of colonists in Liberia.

When Virginia seceded from the Union in 1861, St. George's Episcopal Church withdrew from the Protestant Episcopal Church of the United States and joined the PEC of the Confederate States of America. During the Civil War, Fredericksburg was occupied eleven times by Confederate and Union forces. The war had a profound effect on St. George's. During the Battle of Fredericksburg, the church was struck at least twenty-five times by artillery fire. Despite the church being a place of worship, Union troops looted it, stealing the four-piece communion set. It would take seventy-four years before all the pieces of the set were returned. The building was used as Fredericksburg's largest Union hospital in 1862 and 1864. Many believe that the pain and suffering from the injured and dying were absorbed into the building itself. In 1863, the church was the location of a mass revival where Confederate soldiers found spiritual succor after witnessing the horrors of war.

During Reconstruction, services were held in the basement until the building could be restored. By 1870, the building had been made fully operational again to serve its congregants. Though offered to white and Black parishioners, services were segregated by the vestry, a practice that would continue until 1954. In 1907, the first stained-glass window was dedicated to Mary Ball Washington by the Daughters of the American Revolution (DAR). Throughout the first half of the twentieth century, more stained-glass windows were erected in the memory of parishioners. Three of the windows were designed by the Louis Comfort Tiffany Company.

The Reverend Thomas Faulkner was appointed as rector in 1946, and under his stewardship he confronted racial inequality at the church. Following the Supreme Court's unanimous ruling in *Brown v. Board of Education* that segregation was unconstitutional, Reverend Faulkner informed the church vestry that his "God and Savior opposes segregation in any form and…for me, therefore, the position that I take on segregation is, in the last analysis, a test of my faith in Jesus Christ and God almighty." In accordance with his faith, Reverend Faulkner desegrated St. George's Episcopal Church. Throughout the remainder of the twentieth century and into the twenty-first, St. George's Episcopal Church has confronted social issues, including allowing women to become vestry members and rectors. In 1992, St. George's hosted a World AIDS Day observance and in its statement of welcoming includes all people regardless of creed, race, nationality or sexuality.

In recent years, St. George's Episcopal Church has confronted the churches connection to slavery. On February 16, 2013, the Reverend James C. Dannals hosted a community service titled "From Repentance to Hope: A Service of Remembrance, Celebration and Witness in Commemoration of the 150th Anniversary of the Emancipation Proclamation." The service was conducted by Bishop Jefferts Schori, and during the liturgy, the church repented for its past role of maintaining and supporting slavery. Following the service, community members marched to the Fredericksburg Slave Auction Block, which was then located at its original site at the corner of William and Charles Streets, and then traveled to the rose garden of the Fredericksburg Area Museum for the dedication of *Jubilation* by Ayokunle Odeleye.

A tour of St. George's Episcopal Church is not complete without a tour of the cemetery that is part of the church complex. Laid out in 1728, the cemetery allowed congregants a burial place in consecrated ground. The headstone of John Jones, who died in 1752, is the oldest surviving headstone. William Paul, the brother of John Paul Jones, was a tailor in Fredericksburg and upon his death in 1774 was buried in St. George's Cemetery. Another notable interment in St. George's Cemetery is Martha Washington's father, Colonel John Dandridge, who died suddenly while visiting Fredericksburg in 1756. Before the American Revolution, George Washington paid to have a simple marker placed over his father-in-law's grave. "Here lied interred the Body of Colonel John Dandridge of New Kent County who departed this life the 31st day of August 1756, Aged 56 years."

Colonel John Dandridge's marker is modest compared to the more elaborate inscriptions on display in the cemetery. Two years before Dandridge died, Archibald McPherson joined the permanent residents of St. George's Cemetery. His widow had the following inscribed on his headstone:

Here lyes [sic] *the body of ARCHIBALD MCPHERSON born in the County of Murray in North Britain [Scotland], who died August the 17, 1754 Aged 49 years. He was judicious, a lover of learning, openhearted, generous and sincere. Devout without ostentation, disdaining to cringe to vice in any station. Friend to good men, an affectionate husband. "A heap*

The grave of Colonel John Dandridge, the father of Martha Washington, in St. George's Episcopal Church cemetery. Dandridge died suddenly while on a trip to Fredericksburg. George Washington paid for the grave marker in the 1770s. *Author's photo.*

of dust alone remains of Thee 'Tis all thou art, and all the proud shall be." Elizabeth, his disconsolate widow, as a testimony of their mutual affection, erected this monument to his memory.

Another fascinating inscription is on the headstone of George Richardson and his daughter Nancy. George Richardson was a stonecutter who died suddenly in 1807; his young daughter had died five years earlier. Following his death a beautiful headstone was erected for father and daughter:

Sacred to the memory of GEORGE RICHARDSON STONE CUTTER who was killed by an accident May 12 1807: Aged 45 years. Stay, passenger, thy step, reflect awhile: Tho now in health and vigour [sic] *thou may smile Tomorrow's fun thy obsequies may see The silent grave may then thy mansion be. Then seek in life God's favour* [sic] *to passes And to thy soul secure eternal happiness.*

Nancy daughter of the said George Richardson and Lucy his wife died May 29ᵗʰ 1802: aged 14 months. Jesus said, "Suffer little children, and forbid them not, to come unto me, for such is the Kingdom of heaven."

The last interment in St. George's Cemetery was in 2002: the skeletal remains of three men, two women and a teenage boy uncovered during renovations at Market Square. These were the remains of early colonists, likely from the seventeenth century, who died before the establishment of the church cemetery in 1728. They were reinterred on All Saints Day and memorialized with a ceremony taken from the 1660 Anglican Prayer Book. The Rappahannock Colonial Heritage Society, an eighteenth-century living history association, erected a headstone for the unknown colonists.

The stories of ghosts at St. George's Episcopal Church date to the mid-nineteenth century, making the church one of the oldest haunted buildings in Fredericksburg. The first documented report occurred in 1858, three years before the Civil War. During this period, Americans were fascinated by ghosts and spirits, as the new religion of Spiritualism was gripping the nation. Spiritualism professed that it was possible to contact and speak with the dead. Mediums conducted séances in parlors across the country, and many Americans openly shared their encounters with ghosts. It was in this heightened climate that Fredericksburg resident Ella McCarty encountered the forlorn specter of a woman in white praying at the altar.

According to the tale that Ella McCarty passed down to her children, it was a dark night when she went to St. George's Episcopal Church for choir

People passing the cemetery at St. George's Episcopal Church have reported seeing shadowy figures walking through the cemetery. *Author's photo.*

practice. In 1858, McCarty was seventeen years old. As was proper for the Victorian era, McCarty was not alone when she arrived at the church; she was being chaperoned by Marshall Hall, who managed the Sunday school at the church. Hall was a beloved figure at St. George's, and one of the stained-glass windows at the church is dedicated to his memory. McCarty and Hall had arrived early for practice and found that the only person at the church was the organist. The church was dark, with only a dim light burning in the choir loft, which at this time was located over the church vestibule. Hall and the organist went in search of the church sexton to find more lamps. The sexton was responsible for the upkeep of the church.

While McCarty was waiting for Hall and the organist to return with more light, she ascended the stairs to the choir loft and sat down to view the church below. It was then that McCarty realized that there was a woman kneeling at the altar rail. The woman appeared to be dressed in white with a veil over her face. At first, McCarty thought she was watching a flesh-and-blood person. It was only after watching the woman for several minutes that she realized the woman was a ghost. Despite seeing a ghost,

McCarty was not frightened but continued to watch in fascination. The ghost then rose from the altar rail, turned and looked up at McCarty with a sad expression. It seemed as if the ghost was aware of McCarty's presence. Moved by what she had seen, McCarty started to call out to the ghostly woman to see if she could help, but before she could utter a sound, the woman disappeared.

Ella McCarty was so moved by what she had seen that for the rest of her life she would freely discuss her encounter. McCarty remained in Fredericksburg, and in 1862, met her husband, Dr. Hugh McDonald Martin, during the Battle of Fredericksburg. Hugh Martin was born in 1828 in Scotland and had immigrated to Canada and then moved to Louisiana before the Civil War. During the war, Martin was appointed surgeon of the Fifth Louisiana Infantry. During the Battle of Fredericksburg, McCarty evacuated from her home at 307 or 305 Caroline Street and sought shelter near Prospect Hill and the Belvoir estate. It was here that Martin first spotted Ella McCarty's "golden curls." The couple fell in love and married in July 1863 after the Battle of Gettysburg. They would have five children. After the war, Dr. Martin set up a medical practice in Fredericksburg. Hugh and Ella McCarty Martin died in 1904 and are buried in the Fredericksburg Cemetery. In the twentieth century, Ella's daughters Katherine MacDonald Martin Seddon and Anne Gilmer Martin Stoffregen shared their mother's ghost story with paranormal researcher Margurite DuPont Lee, who published it in her book *Virginia Ghosts*. Lee's version of the story is the definitive account, and it appears that the woman in white that Ella McCarty saw in 1858 has not been seen since. Perhaps the ghostly woman wanted only to be seen and acknowledged and that allowed her to find the peace that she was looking for.

Though the ghostly woman in white has not been seen since 1858, paranormal activity is still rumored to be occurring at St. George's Episcopal Church. In his book *Civil War Ghost Trails: Stories from America's Most Haunted Battlefields*, historian Mark Nesbitt interviewed Fredericksburg police officers who encountered strange things while investigating the church. Officers with the Fredericksburg Police Department are called occasionally to St. George's in the middle of the night to sweep the building to make sure that there was not an intruder after finding the church unlocked. According to the police, their police K-9s were nervous inside the building, especially at the door that leads to the balcony. One veteran officer asserted that there were not many police officers who did not have an experience in the building. Officers have reported hearing footsteps walking through the sanctuary and hear

The grave of William Paul, the brother of John Paul Jones. Paul was a successful tailor before his death in 1774, and his brother came to Fredericksburg to settle his estate. *Author's photo.*

benches creaking as if someone had sat down in a pew. Upon investigation, no one living could be found. A city employee who used to set the clock in St. George's spire said he saw something strange and uncanny at the altar during a visit to the church.

Not everyone who worships at the church believes in the stories. Former rector Reverend Charles Sydor, who preached at St. George's from 1972 to 2003, stated,

> *I never had a run in with a ghost, but occasionally one of the pew doors would pop open with no one near. I would attribute that to the vibration of an old building from traffic outside, but Elizabeth Roberson, our secretary, always said it was Hattie Tackett the ghost. She also spoke of numbers popping off the hymn boards when no one had been near. Well, who knows?*

Another longtime church employee, Elizabeth Roberson, who served as church secretary for thirty-five years, remembered an encounter she had. Roberson was alone in the church prior to the funeral of a well-known congregant. The casket of the deceased had been brought into the church, and Roberson was ensuring that everything was in place. Roberson knew the deceased, and she stated that the person started talking to her. Whatever the person said to her, Roberson did not remember, but she did remember quickly finishing her tasks and hurrying back to her office.

The church is not the only place on the property that is haunted. Strange things have been encountered in the cemetery. One day the caretaker was working in the cemetery when he felt someone come up behind him and tap him on the shoulder, but when he turned around, no one was there. The present church cemetery is not the original size. In the eighteenth and nineteenth centuries, the cemetery was much larger, but when the church was expanded in 1849, it necessitated building over part of the original cemetery. Some of the graves were relocated, but most of the graves were left in place with the new wing built over it. One must wonder if the occupants of those graves are unhappy over having a building erected over them. People have reported seeing figures in white walking back and forth in the cemetery. Making these sightings compelling is that these figures have been seen both in the day and at night. Are these the ghosts of those buried in the cemetery or spirits of Civil War soldiers?

The ghostly outlines of Civil War soldiers have been captured in photographs taken during ghost tours. Were these Union soldiers who were treated at the church during the Battle of Fredericksburg or the spirits of Confederate soldiers who worshiped and were spiritually saved at the church during the revival of 1863? It appears that we will never know for sure. In 2009, a paranormal investigation was held at St. George's, but the investigators were unable to detect any activity. A visit to St. George's Episcopal Church is a moving experience. I highly recommend a visit to see the architectural beauty of the main church and the stained-glass windows. The cemetery features the oldest surviving headstones in Fredericksburg and serves as a silent witness to significant moments in American history. If there are any ghosts at St. George's, they are peaceful ones.

5
THE CHIMNEYS

L ocated on the corner of Caroline and Charlotte Streets is a handsome building known as The Chimneys. Originally built as a residence, The Chimneys is currently a restaurant known as Billiken's Smokehouse at The Chimneys. The structure received its unique nickname due to the two prominent stone chimneys that flank the building at each end. Built between 1771 and 1773, the structure is a testament to the architectural styles of the Georgian period with decorative woodwork moldings, millwork and paneling; an impressive mantelpiece; and carved door and window frames. Constructed when Fredericksburg was a major port city on the Rappahannock River, The Chimneys' hipped roof was built with the same techniques that were common in the construction of ship's hulls. Along with its architectural beauty, The Chimneys is also well known as one of Fredericksburg's most haunted buildings.

Though the early history of the building is unclear, recent research by the University of Mary Washington's Department of Historic Preservation has concluded that The Chimneys was likely built by Charles Yates in the early 1770s. Yates sold the property to John Glassel, who was a wealthy merchant. Born in Galloway, Scotland, to a prominent Lowland family, Glassel immigrated to Virginia in 1756 with his brother Andrew Glassel. John Glassel became a successful merchant and trader in Virginia. The source of Glassel's wealth was trading tobacco grown by the labor of enslaved men, women and children. Glassel's elegant townhouse testified to his wealth and privilege in colonial Fredericksburg. During the Revolutionary War, Glassel sided with the Loyalists and returned to Scotland in 1775.

A wealthy man, John Glassel purchased an estate in 1779 he called Long Niddry House in Haddington, Scotland. Before leaving Fredericksburg, Glassel deeded his American property, including The Chimneys, to his brother Andrew, who remained in the colonies and supported the Patriots. John Glassel remained in Scotland for the remainder of his life and married Helen Buchan on November 18, 1780. The couple's only child, Joanna "Joan" Glassel, was born on June 7, 1796. In 1804, a friend, Walter Colquhoun, wrote a revealing letter to another friend, Daniel Grinnan, who was living in Fredericksburg. Regarding John Glassel, Colquhoun wrote:

Last month I went on a visit to my old friend, Mr. Glassel, and passed eight days with him at Long Niddry, where I was treated with much friendship and hospitality....You may believe we talked much of Virginia affairs.... Mrs. G. is an amiable, well informed woman—active, industrious, extremely attentive to her husband and to his domestic concerns. Their daughter and only child, about eight years of age, a fine looking, healthy, promising girl—she will have a handsome fortune.

The Chimneys was built in the early 1770s and was the home of John Glassel, a successful Scottish merchant. Reports of the house being haunted date to before the Civil War. *Author's photo.*

John Glassel died in 1806 and left his considerable fortune, earned from the labor of enslaved Blacks in Virginia to his daughter, Joanna Glassel. Because of her wealth, Joanna was able to marry into the British aristocracy when she wed Lord John Douglas Henry Campbell, 7th Duke of Argyll.

In the nineteenth century, The Chimneys went through several owners. One notable resident was Ellen "Nell" Lewis Herndon Arthur (1837–1880), the wife of President Chester A. Arthur, who lived in the house as a child. The house was restored in the twentieth century and was used as a rental property and as a museum before becoming a restaurant. Since the 1980s, a succession of restaurants have used the building. In 1982, The Chimneys was renovated and repainted to its original colors, giving visitors a glimpse of what it would have appeared like during the colonial era. Today, visitors come to marvel at the beautiful woodwork and sample delicious barbecue. But amid the clinking of cutlery, spirits from the past can still be felt at The Chimneys.

The Chimneys has had a reputation of being haunted since the mid-nineteenth century. Dr. Brodie Stachan Herndon (1810–1886), who lived in the house before the Civil War, declared that The Chimneys was haunted. Born in Fredericksburg, Herndon was a graduate of the University of Maryland. He returned to Fredericksburg in 1843 and opened a successful medical practice. Herndon lived in The Chimneys with his wife, Lucy Ellen Hansborough, and the couple raised their nine children in the house. Dr. Herndon was a respected member of the community and served as a vestryman at St. George's Episcopal Church. During the Civil War, Herndon was appointed as the chief surgeon for the Confederate army hospitals in Richmond, Virginia. Herndon did not return to The Chimneys at the end of the war; instead of reopening his practice in Fredericksburg, Herndon joined his wife and daughters in Savannah, Georgia. While he lived in The Chimneys, Herndon believed that the house was haunted. Herndon recorded doorknobs turning by themselves and doors opening and closing on their own. Herndon shared his experiences with his friends and neighbors.

In the 1930s, paranormal researcher Marguerite DuPont Lee visited The Chimneys and recorded the stories connected to the building. Unfortunately, Lee did not detail much about her sources for her stories. But she did record some intriguing accounts of the friendly spirits that continued to call The Chimneys home. In the parlor, residents heard a harp being played and a woman singing a tune long out of fashion. It appeared that the ghosts appreciated music, as one evening a young woman was in the parlor playing the piano and singing along to the tune that she was playing. She was alone in the parlor, as her family were sitting on the porch enjoying the fine weather. The woman heard the front door open and close and footsteps in the hall. She addressed the person in the hallway but received no answer. She called out, "Who is trying to frighten me?" but received no answer, though she heard a person come down the hall and enter the parlor where she was playing the piano. She then heard footsteps cross the parlor and felt a person sit down next to her on the piano bench. Her spectral companion then placed a hand on her shoulder. This was too much for her, and she left the room to join her family on the porch.

Lee also included a story about the time one of the owners encountered a ghost in her son's bed. One night, the owner's son went to bed early. His older brothers were at a dance, and he was the only child in the house. His parents were also home and went to bed shortly after their son. It was a chilly night, and the mother was concerned that her son was cold. The mother went to the linen closet and retrieved a heavier blanket to place on her son's bed. She entered her son's room and was surprised to see another boy sleeping peacefully next to her son. She assumed that her son let a friend spend the night and had forgotten to tell her. It was not uncommon for her sons to invite friends over, and many had spent the night at The Chimneys. The next morning when her son came down for breakfast, she asked him who his friend was, as she did not recognize him. Her son was puzzled, as he had not invited anyone to spend the night. Convinced that she had seen a second boy in her son's bed, she went upstairs and found the distinct impression that a second person had slept in the bed. It remained unknown who the spectral guest was.

Residents of The Chimneys have also experienced premonitions while living in the house. One day, one of the residents saw her uncle standing in her room. Her uncle had been ailing for some time, and she was shocked, as her uncle appeared to be in perfect health. This appeared to be a crisis apparition, as three days later, her uncle died. Since The Chimneys has become a restaurant, the spirit of a young boy has been seen on the second floor. Legend states that a young boy died after falling over the balcony. Could this have been the mysterious boy the woman saw in her son's bed so many years ago? Apparently, the ghost does not like a door being closed on the second floor, as staff will frequently find it open after having closed it the night before. The little boy is not the only ghost seen in the building, as witnesses have also seen the ghost of a little girl and a grown woman. It is unclear who these people were and why they are continuing to haunt the building.

One other ghost of note has been encountered in the building. His story illustrates the cruelty of slavery and how this sin still haunts the South. In 2006, paranormal researcher and author Mark Nesbitt encountered the ghost of a Black man named Nicodemus who was detected in the cellar of The Chimneys by a medium. According to Nesbitt, Nicodemus was able to tell the medium that he was waiting in the cellar for a woman named Miss Hattie who had papers that he needed. Without the necessary papers, Nicodemus could not leave, and he had been waiting for over one hundred years. From this description, Nicodemus was likely an enslaved worker who was seeking his freedom through the Underground Railroad.

Though there are no records that lists The Chimneys as a safe house on the Underground Railroad, Fredericksburg was a major stop for freedom seekers on their way to the North and Canada. Something must have gone wrong on Nicodemus's journey, resulting in his death, and he had become trapped in the cellar of The Chimneys. Determined to offer relief to a spirit in need, Nesbitt spoke to Nicodemus and told him that he was free and did not need papers to travel. After speaking to Nicodemus, Nesbitt felt a cold spot on his arm that lasted about five seconds. The cold spot was then replaced by a feeling of warmth. The medium took this as a sign that Nicodemus had crossed over to the other side—as a free man.

I highly recommend that you pay a visit to The Chimneys. The food is delicious, and the atmosphere of dining in a fine colonial mansion is unparalleled. Also, if you are lucky, you just might glimpse the ghostly little boy that roams the halls. And perhaps that harp music playing softly in the background is not coming from a modern sound system but from a faraway time. Also, please remember Nicodemus and the other souls who died while seeking their freedom. I pray that Nicodemus has found his freedom in a better place than the earthly one that held him in bondage.

6

KENMORE

At 1201 Washington Avenue stands Kenmore, an elegant Georgian mansion finished in 1775. Kenmore was the home of Fielding and Betty Washington Lewis and was supposed to be a grand mansion where members of the Virginia gentry could be entertained. The house was outfitted with the finest furniture and had indoor carpeting and wallpaper. On the first floor, three rooms have decorative plaster that are among the finest examples in Virginia. Fielding and Betty Lewis were devoted to the Patriot cause and poured their financial capital into the Revolutionary War; in the process, Fielding Lewis lost his fortune and his health in support of his country. According to legend, the unhappy spirit of Fielding Lewis still roams Kenmore's halls.

Fielding Lewis was born at Warner Hall in Gloucester County on July 7, 1725. Members of the gentry class, his father, John Lewis IV was a merchant and planter, and his mother, Frances Fielding, was the only heir to the wealthy planter Henry Fielding. Sadly, his mother died in childbirth when he was six years old. Fielding was raised by his father and his stepmother, Priscilla Churchill Carter, who was a wealthy widow, which increased the wealth of the Lewis family. Through his marriage to the wealthy and politically powerful Carter family, John Lewis was appointed to the Virginia Council of State.

Fielding Lewis took over his father's store in Fredericksburg in 1747. In 1749, John Lewis constructed a one-story, front-gable, three-bay brick Georgian-style store. The Lewis Store still stands, a testament to the

A Civil War cannonball embedded into the wall of Kenmore. During the Battle of Fredericksburg, Kenmore was struck by Union artillery fire and used as a hospital in 1864. *Author's photo.*

craftsmanship employed in constructing the building. Lewis was a successful merchant and added to his fortune through land speculation and was an investor in bank stocks. On October 18, 1746, Fielding Lewis married his second cousin Catherine Washington. The couple would have three children: John, Frances and Warner. Only their eldest son, John Lewis, lived to adulthood. Catherine Lewis died on February 19, 1750, from complications related to childbirth.

Following the death of his wife, Fielding Lewis courted Betty Washington, who was also his and Catherine Washington Lewis's second cousin. Betty Washington was born on June 20, 1733, at Pope's Creek in Westmoreland County to Augustine and Mary Ball Washington. When Betty was a toddler, she moved with her family to her father's largest plantation, Little Hunting Creek (now known as Mount Vernon). At the age of five, she moved again to Home House (Ferry Farm), where she would live until the age of sixteen. In 1743, her father, Augustine Washington, died, leaving the young child with a dowry of £400 and two enslaved Black women. At the age of ten, Betty became an enslaver. Her mother, Mary, ensured that she had the proper education befitting a member of the gentry. Betty learned how to run a house, care for children and entertain guests. She also mastered necessary skills for a Virginian woman such as fine embroidery, dancing and horsemanship.

After the death of Catherine Lewis, Betty Washington had been helping Fielding Lewis care for his young children. Lewis frequently visited Ferry Farm and proposed marriage to Betty Washington. The couple married, likely at Ferry Farm, on May 7, 1750, a month before Betty's seventeenth birthday. Though the marriage was born out of necessity, Fielding and Betty did fall in love and were a devoted couple for the thirty-one years they were married. Adding to the two surviving children from Lewis's first marriage, Betty gave birth to eleven children. As was typical for the era, only six of her children reached adulthood.

In the early 1770s, Fielding Lewis began construction of the plantation house that would become known as Kenmore. The house was designed by John Ariss to be a showplace for Lewis's wealth and status in the community. Along with being a successful merchant and landowner, Lewis also served as the justice of the peace in Spotsylvania County, a vestryman of St. George's Episcopal Church and in the Virginia House of Burgesses from 1760 to 1769. To build his home, Lewis imported sixty indentured servants who served as craftsmen and would oversee the labor of his enslaved workers who built the home. The main bedchamber, dining room and drawing room were decorated with fine plaster by a craftsman known only as the Stucco Man. Likely an indentured servant, the Stucco Man was also employed by George Washington to decorate the little dining room at Mount Vernon. After the Lewises moved in, George Washington was a frequent visitor.

The Lewises moved to Kenmore in the fall of 1775. At that time, Kenmore was located on the outskirts of Fredericksburg and comprised 1,300 acres, and the property was connected to the home of Mary Washington by a pathway. Fielding and Betty Lewis were cared for by the labor of enslaved Black men, women and children. It was through the tobacco economy that slavery supported that Fielding Lewis made his fortune. Fielding Lewis's relationship with slavery is complicated—though he was an enslaver, Lewis supported the education of enslaved children. In the early 1760s, Reverend James Marye Jr., the rector of St. George's Episcopal Church, recruited Lewis to assist him in opening a Bray School in Fredericksburg. Founded in 1724 by Reverend Thomas Bray, an English Anglican minister, Bray Schools were intended to educate enslaved children. After a Bray School was built in Williamsburg, Benjamin Franklin, who helped the associates of the Reverend Bray in the colonies, suggested that a school should be built in central Virginia.

Fredericksburg was selected, and Fielding Lewis was recruited to assist in operating the school. Despite being an enthusiastic supporter of the project, Lewis found it difficult to convince his neighbors to enroll their enslaved workers in the school. The associates hoped that thirty pupils would be enrolled, but upon the school's opening in April 1765, only seventeen children were enrolled. In a letter to the associates, Fielding complained that "as soon as they could read tolerably to attend in the House of Proprietors, or to take care of the Younger Negros in the Familys [sic] to which they belong" the children were pulled out of the school. The Fredericksburg Bray School closed in the winter of 1769–70 due to low attendance. In 1772, Fielding Lewis wrote another letter to the associates explaining why the school failed. He explained that his white slaveholding neighbors feared an educated and informed enslaved population.

Fielding and Betty Lewis were committed to the Patriot cause during the American Revolution. Fielding Lewis had some military training, as he was elected colonel in the Spotsylvania militia in February 1758. Though he was a colonel, Fieldling Lewis never saw combat. In 1775, Fielding Lewis and Charles Dick were tasked by the third Revolutionary Convention to establish a weapons manufactory in Fredericksburg. Though they were tasked with building the manufactory, the state government did not grant enough funds to maintain the factory. To keep the factory operating, Fielding and Betty Lewis were forced to use their own funds. By the end of the war, Fielding Lewis had lost $7,000 of his own money in the gun manufactory. The factory did produce the necessary arms, as by 1777, the Fredericksburg Gun Manufactory produced about twenty muskets a week. Despite the success in producing arms, the factory never made a profit for Lewis and Dick. Along with running the gun manufactory, Fielding Lewis also built and equipped several ships for Virginia's navy that patrolled the Rappahannock River.

By 1779, the stress of the war and his financial troubles had started to affect Fielding Lewis's health. In a letter to Lord Fairfax in November 1779, General George Washington referenced "the declining state of Col. Lewis' health." As he was likely suffering from tuberculosis at this time, the Lewis family traveled to Berkley Springs, Virginia (now West Virginia) in the summer of 1779. Before the Revolutionary War, Berkley Springs was a popular vacation spot for the gentry, who traveled to the mountain town during the summer to escape the heat and summer illnesses that plagued Virginia during the eighteenth century. Water from the natural springs was believed to have healing properties. The Lewises vacationed every summer at Berkley Springs and would typically stay for a month before returning to Fredericksburg. In June 1779, Betty and Fielding made their annual pilgrimage, but instead of staying for a month, they spent the entire summer in Berkley Springs and returned to Fredericksburg in September 1779.

Upon his return to Fredericksburg, Fielding Lewis's health continued to decline. For the first time in his life, Lewis was unable to help his brother-in-law George Washington with a request for assistance. "My bad state of health prevents my paying that attention," Fielding sadly wrote to Washington. Fielding Lewis traveled to Berkely Springs again in the summer of 1780 but was unable to find relief for his symptoms. By the fall of 1780, he was an invalid at Kenmore and was unable to attend to his business pursuits or the gun foundry.

The spring of 1781 was a nervous time for the city of Fredericksburg and the extended Washington family. The British army had turned its sights toward the southern colonies, and General Lord Cornwallis invaded Virginia. Word reached Fredericksburg that the British intended to destroy the gunnery and ironworks. General George Weedon was tasked with evacuating Mary Washington and the Lewis family. In June 1781, Fielding and Betty Washington Lewis, their children and Mary Washington traveled to Frederick County, Virginia (now West Virginia), to the residence of Fielding Lewis Jr. The journey was arduous, and shortly after their arrival, Samuel Washington, who lived nearby, died from tuberculosis.

While in Frederick County, Fielding Lewis's health declined rapidly, and he was unable to travel back to Fredericksburg after the British threat subsided. In December 1781, Fielding Lewis died at the age of fifty. The exact date of his death and his place of burial are unknown. An 1826 letter written by Robert Lewis to his sister Betty Lewis Carter states that their father was buried in Frederick County.

Betty Washington Lewis returned to Fredericksburg as a widow. Her husband's estate was in debt, and her home was mortgaged. For the remainder of her life, Betty unsuccessfully attempted to settle her husband's estate and collect the funds that were owed to him for maintaining the gun foundry. After the American Revolution, Betty continued to oversee her plantation and helped care for her mother, Mary Washington. Sometime in the mid-1780s, Mary Washington was diagnosed with breast cancer, and by 1787, she was too ill to manage her properties. In 1787, Betty's health also began to decline. In 1789, Mary Washington died at the age of eighty. Betty was devastated, and her older children were concerned about their mother's health. Because President George Washington was in New York and could not return to Fredericksburg to oversee his mother's estate, Betty Lewis oversaw her mother's burial and the settlement of her estate.

For the remainder of her life, Betty Washington Lewis struggled financially. To support herself, she hired out her enslaved workers and took in her orphaned niece Harriot Washington. Along with her niece, Betty Lewis also cared for her step granddaughters. She even opened a boarding school at Kenmore and sold some of the additional plantation acreage. Despite her best efforts, the school did not produce enough funds to keep her afloat at Kenmore. Two years before her death, Betty left Kenmore and moved to a smaller farm twelve miles south of Fredericksburg. While visiting her daughter Betty Lewis Carter at Western View, in Orange County, Virginia, Betty Washington Lewis died on March 31, 1797, at the age of sixty-four. Following her death, her son George Washington Lewis wrote to his brother Fielding Lewis Jr. that they had lost "the dearest and best of women."

After Betty's death, her stepson John Lewis inherited Kenmore per the dictates of his father's will. The expense of maintaining the plantation was too great for John Lewis to afford, and he sold Kenmore to John James Maund. With the funds he received from the sale of Kenmore, John Lewis moved his family to Kentucky. Lewis never returned to Virginia and died in Kentucky in 1825. Maund owned Kenmore for two years and sold the property to Seth Barton in 1799. Barton owned Kenmore until 1815, when the property was sold to John Thornton, who owned it for only four years. Thornton sold Kenmore to the next major owner, Samuel Gordon. The Gordon family would own Kenmore for twenty-nine years.

Samuel Gordon was born in Galloway, Scotland, in the 1750s. In 1780, Gordon immigrated to Virginia. After the Revolutionary War, Gordon moved to Falmouth in 1786 and became a successful merchant. At the age of thirty-nine, Gordon married Susan "Susanna" Fitzhugh Knox in 1798. The couple would have ten children. In 1811, Gordon inherited his father's estate in Scotland. This made Samuel Gordon a very wealthy man. To reflect his wealth and status in the community, Gordon purchased Fielding Lewis's home along with two hundred acres of the former Lewis plantation from John Thornton in December 1819.

It was during Gordon's ownership of the Lewis home that the property was named Kenmore as tribute to his Scottish heritage. Samuel and Susanna Gordon lived at Kenmore with their six sons and three daughters. The two hundred acres that the Gordons owned included Meditation Rock, where Mary Washington frequently visited to pray and was buried in 1789. Upset that the location of Mary Washington's grave was unmarked, New York philanthropist Silas K. Burrows funded the construction of a monument in the 1830s. But due to an economic reversal, Burrows was unable to provide the necessary funds to complete the project. For decades, the Mary Washington Monument sat unfinished. During the Civil War, soldiers on both sides used the monument for target practice. In the early 1890s, the original monument was torn down, and a new monument was completed in 1894. The monument is not erected over Mary Washington's grave but was built to commemorate the legacy of Mary Washington as the mother of George Washington near a place where she frequently visited during her life and was eventually buried. Near the Mary Washington Monument is the Gordon family cemetery.

Samuel Gordon lived at Kenmore until his death in 1843. Following her husband's death, Susanna Gordon inherited the property. In 1848, Samuel's son William Gordon and his wife, Eliza Fitzhugh Gordon, moved to Kenmore. William and Eliza Gordon lived at Kenmore for a decade. Two years before the Civil War, the Gordons sold Kenmore to Franklin Slaughter in 1859 for $25,000. Before selling the property, William Gordon stipulated

Kenmore was the home of Fielding and Betty Washington Lewis, the sister of George Washington. Fielding Lewis's ghost has been seen pacing the halls. *Author's photo.*

that he had "the right of burying any of his own family in the grave yard on the land." When William Gordon died in 1886, he was buried in the Gordon family cemetery at Kenmore.

During the eighteenth and nineteenth centuries, the wealth of the Lewis and Gordon families came from the labor of enslaved workers. Men, women and children toiled the land, cleaned the mansion and cared for the Lewis and Gordon families. It was only through their labor that Fielding Lewis could afford to maintain 1,300 acres of land. By the mid-nineteenth century, Kenmore had been whittled down to 200 acres, but the plantation was still maintained through chattel slavery.

Franklin Slaughter sold 4.25 acres of Kenmore including the mansion to Mrs. Henningham C. Harrison from Goochland County for $10,000. After Harrison's death in 1861, she left Kenmore to Elizabeth W.H. Gordon of Baltimore. The Civil War came to Kenmore in December 1862 when the house was struck by cannonballs during an artillery battle between Union and Confederate forces. During the battle, Confederate artillery batteries were placed on modern-day Washington Avenue, attracting return fire from Union forces stationed along the Rappahannock River near Chatham. After the Battle of the Wilderness and Spotsylvania Courthouse, Kenmore was used as a hospital for Union soldiers. Conditions within the house were horrific; it is believed that the dining room was used as an operating theater.

Amputated limbs were piled in heaps in the yard, and the dead were lined up on the ground for burial. Inside, the injured lay on the floor in the rooms and the hallways. There were so many people crammed on the floor that it was virtually impossible for the doctors and orderlies to take a step without treading on the injured. Those who had a chance at survival were eventually transported to military hospitals in Washington, D.C. By the end of the war, Kenmore was a shadow of its former self.

After the Civil War, Elizabeth W.H. Gordon sold Kenmore to Levi Beardsley in 1867 for $4,500. It is unknown if Beardsley lived in Kenmore, and he sold the property in 1870 to William Barton. Not much is known about Barton, and he sold the property in 1881 to William Key Howard Sr. Born in Maryland in 1829, Howard was a Confederate soldier and spy who spent most of the war imprisoned. After the war, William Key Howard moved to Fredericksburg with his wife, Clara Randolph Howard, and their three sons: William Jr., Allan and Clarence. The family first resided at Altoona Plantation before moving to Kenmore. By the 1880s, the plaster ceilings were starting to deteriorate, and William Sr. was going to have them taken down. Fortunately, William Jr. convinced his father to let him restore the plaster ceilings and he painstakingly restored the ceilings despite suffering from a back ailment.

In 1887, William Sr. conveyed Kenmore to his namesake for $4,000. William Sr. and Clara Howard continued to live at Kenmore. Despite officially owning Kenmore, William Jr. did not live at the property. In 1895, William Howard Jr. was living in Georgia where he married Florence Lamar Moore. William Jr. and Florence lived in Georgia, where they raised their family. William Key Howard Sr. lived at Kenmore until his death on February 10, 1899. In 1902, William Jr. returned to Virginia with his family, but he did not move back to Fredericksburg, instead settling in Urbana, where he ran an ice plant. The Howard family conveyed the property to Clarence Howard in 1905. For the next nine years, Clarence Howard and his wife lived at Kenmore with various family members and boarders. By March 1914, the Howards had decided to subdivide the property further to settle debts.

Kenmore was purchased by Elmer Grimsley "Peck" Heflin and a business partner for $20,000. Heflin became the sole owner a few years later and wanted to turn what was left of the Kenmore property into a subdivision. He intended to remove the plasterwork from Kenmore and turn the building into apartments. Fortunately, Kenmore was saved from destruction in 1925 by the Kenmore Association, now known as the George Washington Foundation (GWF). Founded by Emily White Fleming and her daughter Annie Fleming Smith, the Kenmore Association recognized that Kenmore was both an architectural and historical landmark. The Garden Club of Virginia helped with the restoration of the gardens and to raise funds for the project inaugurated garden week that is held every year. Today, Historic Kenmore has been lovingly restored by the George Washington Foundation to its circa 1775 appearance when Fielding and Betty Washington Lewis moved into the house. In 1996, the GWF saved Ferry Farm, the boyhood home of George Washington. The original home that George Washington had grown up in had been torn down in the nineteenth century, and the site was endangered by modern development. In 2003, archaeological excavation started at Ferry Farm and resulted in the discovery of the remains of the Washington home in 2006. The Washington Home was rebuilt, opening to the public in 2018.

Though Fielding Lewis has been dead since 1781, his ghost has been seen wandering the halls of his beloved home. The accounts of Kenmore being haunted by the ghost of Fielding Lewis date from the early twentieth century. Fielding Lewis's spirit appears to be troubled, as he is seen sitting at his desk in the main bedchamber studying his account books in distress. He also makes his presence known in other ways, as the tread of heavy footsteps is also heard in the hallway and on the stairs. A friend of mine heard heavy footsteps in the hallway. Activity is also reported on the grounds of Kenmore, as people have also heard a person walking on the gravel walkway leading to the front door followed by the scrape of leather-soled shoes on the sandstone steps and the turning of the doorknob.

The most active room is the main bedchamber that served as Fielding and Betty Washington Lewis's bedroom. Along with being their bedroom, the chamber also served as a private parlor for Betty, where she could entertain family members and close friends. Paranormal researcher Marguerite DuPont Lee recorded an incident that occurred shortly after Kenmore had opened as a museum. Mrs. William Jeffries Chewing was in the main chamber on a hot and sultry day giving a tour to two friends when she suddenly felt a cold draft of air blowing on the back of her head. On such a hot day, this cold spot must have been a relief. Mrs. Chewing told Lee that she remarked to her friends, "I think this is the haunted room." As if to acknowledge her statement, the three women heard a clicking sound, and the wardrobe door flew open.

Fielding Lewis is not the only spirit seen at Kenmore—people have reported seeing the ghosts of Civil War soldiers on the property. The first sightings of spectral soldiers were recorded in October 1870. An account was published in the *Fredericksburg Ledger*:

APPEARANCE OF A GHOST.—The people on the western part of town, near Kenmore, are very much exercised about the appearance of what is supposed to be a ghost in that quarter last Sunday morning between 11 and 12 o'clock. It is said that about that time of day, during the shower of rain, Mr. Mills saw a man crawling on his hands along by the fence dragging his feet after him, as though his legs were paralyzed. He spoke to two ladies standing in the door and asked "What does that mean?" Of course they could not tell him, and Mr. Mills said that he would see, and stepped out to the fence, which was but ten or fifteen feet, by which time the supposed man had passed him some feet. Mr. Mills got over the fence, and started after the man and asked where he was going. The man straightened up on his feet to full height—which was higher than that of a medium seized man—and said in a distinct tone: "I am going down," and vanished from sight. The figure was dressed in the full uniform of a Federal solider, which was clean and apparently new, with the blue overcoat coming down to near his feet. Mr. Mills did not see the face of the man, but the two ladies did, and say the face was a bronze with hard features.

The persons who say they saw this are of undoubted veracity, and although they do not believe in ghosts, they are unable to account for this sudden appearance and mysterious disappearance in broad daylight. It has created quite an excitement in that part of town.

The description of the Union soldier matches the type of uniform that would have been worn during the Battle of Fredericksburg in December 1862. Could this have been the ghost of a solider who died during the battle?

The spirits of Kenmore seem to be residual in nature, as the ghosts of Fielding Lewis and the Civil War soldiers do not interact with the living. Fortunately for Lewis, his ghost seems to be only a memory of when he lived in the house and is not actively trapped on the property. The stress and strain that he experienced, along with the pain suffered by the injured Union soldiers, were so great that remnants were embedded in the very building itself. Under certain conditions, these memories play back like a video recording that the living can occasionally see but not interact with. For all that Fielding and Betty Lewis endured to help the colonies gain independence, I am glad that the haunting is residual. May Fielding Lewis rest in peace, and may his sacrifices be remembered.

7

HAZEL HILL

In 1793, John Minor built for his bride a mansion in Fredericksburg that he named Hazel Hill. The mansion was the center of a plantation encompassing thirty-seven acres of gardens and farmland that stretched from what is now Princess Anne Street to the Rappahannock River. The son of Major John and Elizabeth Cosby Minor, John Minor was born on May 13, 1761, at Topping Castle in Caroline County, Virginia. As a teenager, John was enrolled by his parents in the College of William & Mary in Williamsburg, Virginia. While attending college, Minor became a supporter of the Patriot cause. At the age of fifteen, Minor ran away from school to join the army and fight for his country's independence in the Revolutionary War. Minor enlisted as a private in Nelson's Light-Horse Troop, which was part of "Light-Horse" Harry Lee's command. He served with distinction, and after the war he returned to the College of William & Mary and studied law under George Wythe.

After the completion of his studies, Minor moved to Fredericksburg, where he established a successful law practice and became Fredericksburg's first commonwealth's attorney. Minor was popular with his colleagues and was renowned for "his knowledge of law and his magnetic eloquence" as a speaker. Along with maintaining a law practice, Minor also served as a colonel of the Spotsylvania County militia. During the War of 1812, Minor was appointed by the Virginia legislature as brigadier general in the militia.

In 1786, John Minor married Mary Berkley, who was the daughter of Nelson Berkely and Elizabeth Wormley Carter. Minor took his bride to

Fredericksburg. Sadly, Mary and her infant daughter died in childbirth on October 23, 1787. John Minor had a headstone erected in Airwell Cemetery in Hanover County to mark his wife's grave. The headstone still stands as a testament to his grief. The grieving husband and father commissioned the following inscription:

> *Heres* [sic] *lies the dust of Mary Nelson Minor and her infant who departed this life October 23, 1787. This monument was erected by her husband John Minor to mark to future years the Spot where they were laid. They are gone but we shall meet again.*

In 1793, John Minor married his second wife, Lucy Landon Carter, with whom he had seven children. The Minors lived at Hazel Hill, which he had built for his new family. Minor named his plantation after Hazel Run, a stream that ran through the property. John Minor was devoted to his family and took immense pride in his children.

Minor was also involved in politics, serving in the Virginia General Assembly. While in the General Assembly, Minor introduced two bills in 1782 and 1790 calling for the eradication of slavery in the United States. The first bill in 1782 provided for the "gradual emancipation" of the enslaved. The second bill that Minor introduced in 1790 provided for the "transportation and colonization" to Africa following emancipation. Both bills passed, but no action was taken by the General Assembly. Minor supported colonization and freed his slaves and paid for their transportation to Liberia. It is not known if they stayed in Liberia or returned to the United States.

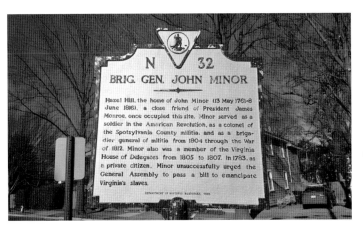

The historical marker for Hazel Hill. In 1816, the ghost of John Minor returned to his beloved home the night he died. *Author's photo.*

In 1790, Minor ran for Congress against his friend James Monroe. Despite losing the election, Minor remained friends with Monroe for the remainder of his life. From 1805 to 1807, Minor served in the Virginia House of Burgesses. In 1816, Minor was a member of Virginia's Electoral College and traveled from Fredericksburg to Richmond. According to legend, Minor was in Richmond to cast his vote for James Monroe in the Electoral College. This is not possible, as Minor died in June, and the election of 1816 was held on Tuesday, November 5, five months after Minor's death. Minor's obituary, published on June 12, 1816, stated that Minor was in Richmond "for the purpose of attending to his professional engagements in the Federal Court, and the Court of Chancery."

Though he had been ill in the days leading up to his death, he appeared to have recovered. "On Thursday last at 1 o'clock, he was in the [chancery] court, in better health and spirits than he usually enjoyed for some time past: a slight indisposition admonished him to retire to his lodgings; the symptoms becoming more violent, medical aid was called in; but the case was not considered as dangerous, on 12 o'clock of Saturday. On the evening of that day he thought himself much better, and seemed to be cheered by the circumstances of his pains having left him," an anonymous friend recorded in John Minor's obituary.

The legend following Minor's death claims that on the night of June 8, 1816, Minor attended a dinner given in honor of the Electoral College by the citizens of Richmond. As part of the dinner, Minor was asked to deliver an address to celebrate the election of Monroe. While in the process of giving his speech, John Minor collapsed and died suddenly from a stroke. It is unclear what Minor was doing when he died; his obituary published in the *Richmond Enquirer* does not mention the Electoral College. According to the obituary, Minor died suddenly in the evening. "He expired without a struggle, without a groan," the obituary stated.

Back in Fredericksburg, John Minor's family were preparing for dinner, unaware of the tragedy that had befallen them. Yet according to Minor's children, in their father's last moments, his spirit returned one last time to the family and home that he loved so much.

One hundred years later, John Minor's granddaughter Mary Isabella Blackford recorded the story. "My mother [Mary Minor Blackford] never did tell me this ghost story at all. I never heard it till after I was grown....My grandmother [Lucy Minor] had kept it a dead secret for forty years. The servants had strict orders not to mention it in Fredericksburg or anywhere. In those days servants had to mind. As far as I know, they never did tell it," Blackford wrote. It is unclear why Lucy Minor prevented her servants from discussing the strange events that occurred at Hazel Hill the night John Minor died. It is possible that Lucy Minor did not want it bandied about town that a ghost had been seen in her home.

Though Lucy Minor and Mary Minor Blackford never discussed the ghost sighting, an account of what happened was relayed to Mary Isabella Blackford through interviews with her uncles who were also at Hazel Hill that night. Mary Isabella recorded the story for her nephew Berkeley Minor. According to Mary Isabella Blackford:

> *General Minor was at that time a member of the General Assembly that was meeting in Richmond. My grandmother was not expecting him at all. She was sitting in her dining room at Hazle* [sic] *Hill about 6 o'clock that evening…with her sons, their tutor and my mother, when suddenly the door opened and the butler, an elderly colored man, came in and said, "Mistress, did you know Master had come?" She rose from the table quite excited and said, "No, Ben, I was not expecting General Minor. Where is he?"*
>
> *Then they all followed Ben out in the hall and saw* [General John Minor] *at the lower end and just about to go upstairs. He turned a moment and looked at them and then went on up. He was in full evening dress. They could see his hand on the banister as he went up, and the ruffles at his wrist. Some went upstairs and searched every room but he was no where to be found. The family were all excited and distressed, not knowing what to think.*

Several hours later, a messenger arrived at Hazel Hill from Richmond with a letter detailing John Minor's sudden death. The news of John Minor's death came as a shock to his friends and family.

According to the family, John Minor's spirit appeared not only at his home at Hazel Hill but also at the plantation of his in-laws in King George County. Minor's descendant Charles M. Blackford recorded this story:

> *In regard to the death of General Minor there is retained in the family a well authenticated incident which almost amounts to a ghost story. He died in Richmond…about eleven o'clock at night in the State capitol. The same evening there were assembled around the parlor fire at Cleve, in King George county, a number of the members of his wife's family, among them her brother-in-law, Mr. Wm. McFarland, a lawyer of talents, but*

more given to poetry than to law. He had a mind which would be called "impressionable," and which would make a good "medium." About eleven o'clock he left the room to go to bed, but in a moment returned somewhat alarmed, saying that he had seen General Minor in the gallery up stairs [sic]—yet he was sure it was only his ghost. He was laughed at and told it was only his fancy, so he started out again, but returned with the same story, and then the whole went with him, but not being impressionable, the ghost was not seen. In a few days they learned that the time Mr. McFarland went up stairs [sic] was the hour at which General Minor had died in Richmond. Mr. McFarland's fancies ever afterwards were more esteemed. Of course, there was no ghost, nor was there anything supernatural in McFarland's vision. The art of photography and wireless telegraphy in the physical world prepares us to believe that on a mind peculiarly sensitive, impressions may be made by physical facts at a distance, to which the common mind is absolutely oblivious.

Following his death, John Minor's earthly remains were returned to Fredericksburg; along the route, county courts that were in session adjourned out of respect. Following his funeral at St. George's Episcopal Church, Minor was buried at the family burial ground at Hazel Hill. In 1855, the remains of John Minor and his wife were reinterred in the Fredericksburg Masonic Cemetery. Over the years, Hazel Hill passed through several owners. During the Battle of Fredericksburg in December 1862, Hazel Hill's cupola was used as a sniper's nest by Confederate soldiers. By the twentieth century, the plantation was in shambles, and Hazel Hill was demolished in 1950. All that remains is a historical marker to John Minor and the Hazel Hill apartments—a sad ending to the story of a man who loved his family so much that even death could not stop him from coming home.

8

FREDERICKSBURG BATTLEFIELD

The Battle of Fredericksburg is one of the most overlooked campaigns of the American Civil War. Compared to Gettysburg, Antietam and Vicksburg, the Battle of Fredericksburg is viewed as a campaign that accomplished little for either side. Today, visitors come to the Fredericksburg Battlefield Visitor Center at 1013 Lafayette Boulevard to learn about the battle, watch the National Park Service's introductory video and tour the original Sunken Road. The first time I visited the Fredericksburg Visitor Center as a tourist in 2008, I must admit that I was underwhelmed. Earlier in my vacation, I had spent three days touring Gettysburg and was disappointed that the Fredericksburg battlefield was smaller than what I had seen in Pennsylvania. In my narrowmindedness, I overlooked that, like Gettysburg, the city of Fredericksburg was also part of the battlefield. The battle was not limited to one small patch of land. From December 11 to 15, 1862, the battle engulfed the city and left a permanent scar on the land.

The Battle of Fredericksburg was one of the largest and deadliest battles of the American Civil War, with nearly 200,000 combatants. It was a battle of firsts, from the first opposed river crossing in American military history to the first instance of urban combat in the Civil War. Following the Battle of Antietam, President Abraham Lincoln removed Major General George McClellan from command of the Union army of the Potomac. President Lincoln was frustrated with the grandstanding General McClellan, who had not followed up his victory at the Battle of Antietam by following Confederate general Robert E. Lee's Army of Northern Virginia. Lincoln believed that if McClellan had chased Lee's army, he could have delivered a crippling blow. Rather than pursue the enemy, McClellan decided to rest his battered army. In his place, Lincoln chose Major General Ambrose E. Burnside. A career officer, Burnside felt that he was not up to the job. Burnside inherited an army full of McClellan loyalists, and though he had no political enemies in Washington, D.C., he crucially did not have any allies.

As the new commander of the Army of the Potomac, Burnside drew up an ambitious plan to cut Lee's army off from Richmond, the Confederate capital. The initial campaign started well for the Army of the Potomac; on November 15, 1862, Burnside moved his 100,000-man army out of Warrenton, Virginia. Moving quickly, the army marched thirty-five miles in just two days, arriving in Falmouth. The Union army was poised to cross the Rappahannock River and take Fredericksburg. At that time, Fredericksburg was occupied by only a few hundred Confederates. During the antebellum era, bridges had been built over the Rappahannock River; these bridges had been burned by the Confederates to hinder the enemy. Burnside ordered portable pontoon bridges to be brought up for his army to cross the Rappahannock River. But logistical and bureaucratic wrangling delayed the pontoon bridges' arrival at Falmouth.

While Burnside waited for the pontoons to arrive, Lee was able to move reinforcements into Fredericksburg. The Confederates began to reinforce the area around Marye's Heights, which overlooked Fredericksburg. Lee's forces also entrenched south of Fredericksburg in a line from Prospect Hill to Hamilton's Crossing. The time that the Federals lost waiting for the supply line to catch up to the army would have disastrous consequences. To protect the civilian population, Lee urged that children, women and the elderly should evacuate from the town. Hundreds of civilians fled, leaving their properties in Fredericksburg unprotected from an oncoming army.

On November 25, 1862, the pontoons began to arrive at Falmouth, but logistical issues continued to plague the Army of the Potomac. Finally, on December 11, the engineers began to assemble the pontoon bridges across the Rappahannock River. Work on the bridges began in the foggy predawn hours, but Confederate riflemen who were hiding in buildings along the riverbank opened fire on the engineers. To halt the snipers, Burnside ordered the Union artillery to bombard the town. For four hours, Union artillery fired on Fredericksburg, raining destruction on the town. The few hundred civilians who had remained cowered in fear in their basements and cellars. Fanny White, who was ten years old in December 1862, would remember, "For long hours the only sounds that greeted our ears were the whizzing and moaning of shells and the crash of falling bricks and timber." Virtually every building in town received damage from the bombardment.

The shelling of Fredericksburg failed to dislodge the snipers. After meeting with his officers, Burnside approved of a plan to send a landing party to deal with the snipers and secure a bridgehead in the town. Men from Michigan and Massachusetts landed in town under fire and were successful in dislodging the snipers. The fighting in Fredericksburg on the afternoon of December 11 was brutal, as Union soldiers went door-to-door to root out the snipers. With a bridgehead secured, the Army of the Potomac was able to move regiments across the river. By December 12, the remainder of the Union army had crossed the river and occupied the town. Union troops began to ransack and loot the homes, shops and public buildings of Fredericksburg. Though Burnside ordered that the looting stop, many officers were reluctant to enforce the order.

During the lull in the battle caused by the looting, Lee was able to bring Confederate general Thomas "Stonewall" Jackson's corps into position

A reconstruction of a pontoon bridge on display at Chatham Manor. The Union army used pontoon bridges to move troops across the Rappahannock River in December 1862. *Author's photo.*

around Prospect Hill while the rest of the army under General James Longstreet was left in place at Marye's Heights. To advance, the Union army of 100,000 men would have to dislodge a well-entrenched army made up of 80,000 battle-hardened veteran soldiers. The main assault began on December 13; though the Union army gained initial success against Jackson's corps at Prospect Hill, the lack of coordination stymied the Federals. In Fredericksburg, the Union's advance on Marye's Heights produced unprecedented carnage.

Wave after wave of Union troops charged against Longstreet's well-fortified troops, who were protected by a four-foot-tall stone wall at the Sunken Road. The Sunken Road provided ideal coverage, as years of heavy wagons had caused the road to sink. Behind the wall, the Confederates stood three ranks deep, which produced a constant withering fire on the Union soldiers tasked with charging over open ground. On Marye's Heights, Confederate artillery fired down on the Union army. Despite their best efforts, the Union soldiers were unable to dislodge the Confederates from Marye's Height. By nightfall, seventeen Union brigades had attempted to rout the Confederates. The ground in front of the Sunken Road was littered with dead and dying men. Confederate officers and soldiers were sickened by what they witnessed, and Lee declared, "It is well that war is so terrible. We should grow too fond of it."

By the evening of December 14, it was clear that the battle had ended in a victory for the Confederate army. Realizing that the campaign had ended in defeat, Burnside ordered his army to retreat and return to Falmouth. The homes that lined the Sunken Road, the Stephens House and the Innis House were riddled with bullets. After the war, both houses would become tourist attractions, as people came to view the battle-scarred homes. Casualties for the Union army were high—with 12,653 men killed, wounded or missing—compared to the Confederates, who had 5,309 men killed, wounded or missing. The defeat at Fredericksburg was an embarrassment to the federal government, and six weeks later Burnside was removed from command. After the war, the Fredericksburg National Cemetery opened in 1866 on Marye's Heights, and the Sunken Road comprises the heart of the Fredericksburg National Military Park. Visitors from around the world come to walk and view the place where some of the most intense combat of the Civil War occurred.

It is not surprising that ghost stories are connected to the Sunken Road, as it is estimated that more than two-thirds of the Union casualties sustained during the Battle of Fredericksburg occurred at the Sunken

The wall at the Sunken Road. During the Battle of Fredericksburg, Confederate soldiers used the four-foot-tall wall as entrenchments while raining death down on the charging Union forces. *Author's photo*

Road. Over the years, the ghost of a woman has been seen at the location of the Stephens House and cemetery. All that remains of the Stephens House is the outline of the foundation. In December 1862, Martha Stephens lived in a small house along the Sunken Road with her common-law husband and their two children. Martha Stephens was a rough character who operated a tavern at her home and may have also run a brothel. She was described by a contemporary as "a woman of abandoned character and an outcast of society." Following the battle, Stephens created the legend that she cared for injured Confederate and Union soldiers. Her exploits made her a celebrity, and her house became a tourist attraction. She regaled visitors with stories of her bravery and proudly showed guests her bullet-riddled house. Martha Stephens died in 1888 and was buried next to her home, and the site is marked by a marble urn. In 1913, the Stephens House was destroyed by fire. Today, it is believed that the ghostly woman seen around the Stephens House is Martha Stephens.

Above: All that remains of the Stephens House is the outline of the basement and the family cemetery. Today guests have reported seeing the ghost of Martha Stephens walking around her former home. *Author's photo.*

Opposite, top: The Innis House was at the center of a maelstrom on December 13, 1862. *Author's photo.*

Opposite, bottom: The interior walls of the Innis House are still pockmarked by bullet holes from the Battle of Fredericksburg. Following the war, the Innis House became a tourist attraction. *Author's photo.*

Residents who live around the Sunken Road have claimed to have seen unexplained things at the National Park. These reports have ranged from seeing strange mists to seeing men dressed as Civil War soldiers that appear to be solid until they inexplicably disappear. Also seen floating over the road are blue firefly-like lights that resemble cemetery lights.

The Sunken Road is not the only place in town where ghosts related to the Battle of Fredericksburg are seen or felt. Behind Shiloh New Site Baptist Church at 525 Princess Anne Street, people have heard footsteps of an unseen person wearing brogans with metal heel plates on the soles. Brogans were worn by both Confederate and Union soldiers, and the men would put metal heel plates on the leather-soled shoes to grip the ground better. It is believed that the footsteps belong to the spirits of Union soldiers, as Confederate reenactors feel unwelcomed at the site.

At the Willis House at 1106 Princess Anne Street, a restless Union soldier used to roam the halls until he finally found peace. The Willis House was built sometime in the 1740s by Scottish merchant John Allan. During the Civil War, a Union soldier entered the house and was standing behind one of the double doors in the back hall when a bullet ripped through the door, killing him instantly. The soldier was buried in the garden. According to Barbara Willis, who lived in the house in the late twentieth century, the door that the soldier was hiding behind was plugged and the door was still in use in the hall. For whatever reason, the soldier was not disinterred and moved to the Fredericksburg National Cemetery.

The Willis family came to believe that their house was haunted by the Union soldier. In the 1920s, Marian "Carrie" Willis lived in the house and employed a cook named Nannie. Carrie had playfully named the Union soldier "Yip the Yank." One day when Nannie arrived at the Willis House, she saw a young man enter the house through the side porch. The young man was dressed in the uniform of a Union soldier. At first, Nannie thought that the man was Carrie's brother. Nannie watched the man go upstairs, but after a search for him, the man could not be found. When Nannie was told that she had just seen Yip the Yank, she decided that she would help the lost soul. Nannie went to the garden where the solider was buried and began to pray for the man's soul. After Nannie's prayers, Yip was never seen again in the Willis House. The scars of the Civil War are easily found in Fredericksburg. Nearly every building has a story to tell, and many believe that the spirits of the Union and the Confederate dead still linger.

9
MANNSFIELD

Mannsfield Plantation once stood on the outskirts of Fredericksburg until war and modern development destroyed any vestige of one of the finest plantations in the region. Today the only thing remaining of Mannsfield is the cemetery on a knoll, located on private property. The plantation was built for Mann Page III in 1770 on the banks of the Rappahannock River two miles south of Fredericksburg

Mann Page was born at Rosewell Plantation in Gloucester County, Virginia, in 1749. The Pages were one of the First Families of Virginia, part of the economic and political elite during the colonial period. Mann Page served in the House of Burgesses and participated in the first meeting of the Virginia House of Delegates. During the American Revolution, Page served as a delegate from Virginia in the Continental Congress in 1777. In 1776, Mann Page married Mary Tayloe, and the couple had three children. Mann Page constructed his plantation, Mannsfield, as a replica of Mount Airy, the Tayloe family plantation. The mansion house was built with sandstone blocks and featured two detached wings that were linked to the main house with a circular covered walkway. Mannsfield lay next to Richmond Road (now Routes 2 and 17), which connected Fredericksburg to Richmond. Following his death in 1781, Mann Page was buried in the family cemetery at Mannsfield.

Sometime in the early 1800s, Mannsfield was sold to William Bernard, who moved his family from Belle Grove Plantation in King George County to the sprawling plantation. Bernard had decided to leave Belle

A drawing of Mannsfield, the home of Mann Page. The plantation was accidentally burned to the ground by Confederate soldiers in 1863. *Courtesy of the National Park Service.*

Grove Plantation upon marrying his second wife, Elizabeth Hooe, in 1804. William Bernard died in 1841, and Mannsfield remained in the Bernard family. By 1860, Mannsfield was owned by Arthur Bernard, and the mansion stood in the center of one of Fredericksburg's most prosperous plantations. The plantation consisted of 1,800 acres with thirty outbuildings, where seventy-seven enslaved workers maintained the wealth of the Bernard family.

The Civil War came to Mannsfield in December 1862 during the Battle of Fredericksburg. Fighting occurred on the plantation at Bernard Slave Cabins. Located one and a half miles to the east of the mansion house, Bernard Slave Cabins was a small community of enslaved workers owned by Arthur Bernard. About three dozen men, women and children lived in three two-room cabins with water provided by a stone-lined well; by 1862, there may have been two additional buildings. During the Battle of Fredericksburg, Confederate general Thomas "Stonewall" Jackson placed Confederate artillery on the site of Bernard Slave Cabins to block Federal advancement onto nearby Prospect Hill. To provide a clear vantage point for the artillery, the cabins were torn down, which would create disastrous results for the Confederates.

The fighting at Bernard Slave Cabins on the morning of December 13, 1862, proved to be a bloodbath for the Confederate troops. The Confederate gunners were exposed to enemy fire and were mowed down by Federal troops. To repulse the Federal attackers, Confederate artillery opened fire with Federal artillery batteries returning fire. The Union fire was withering; at one Confederate cannon, a Union ball hit the ammunition chest, causing an explosion. To protect what was left of the Confederate artillery, General Jackson canceled the attack.

The fighting at Bernard Slave Cabins was not the only engagement around the Mannsfield Plantation on December 13, 1862. At Mannsfield and the neighboring plantations Smithfield and the Bend, Union troops gathered before the engagement at Slaughter Pen Farm. The Union army planned a flank attack to cut off the enemy in Fredericksburg by capturing Richmond Road. Due to poorly worded orders, eight thousand Union soldiers gathered to attack more than thirty-eight thousand Confederate troops. The fighting at Slaughter Pen Farm was horrific; despite being severely outnumbered, the Union soldiers put up a valiant fight. For their bravery, five Union soldiers were awarded the Congressional Medal of Honor.

During the battle, Mannsfield served as the headquarters for Union generals William Buel Franklin, John Fulton Reynolds and William Farrar Smith. The mansion house was also struck by cannon fire, causing serious damage. Union general George Dashiell Bayard was mortally wounded at Mannsfield when he was stuck by a piece of shrapnel from a Confederate artillery round in the leg. Tragically, doctors were unable to staunch the wound and Bayard died the next day due to massive blood loss. Following the Union retreat from Fredericksburg, Mannsfield was used by the Confederates. Mannsfield was accidentally buried to the ground by Confederate soldiers in April 1863.

Following the Civil War, the only part of Mannsfield that was still standing was the south wing dependency—a lonely sentinel of a once grand plantation. After the war, the ruins of Mannsfield gained a reputation for being haunted by the spirits of Civil War soldiers. In the early twentieth century, the owner of Mannsfield, William Bernard Sr., wrote to paranormal researcher Marguerite DuPont Lee:

The colored people born and raised here could never be induced to go to the grove or near the ruins after dark, declaring ghosts commenced to walk around at night. Of course, nobody paid any attention to them. Finally, some years later the farm was tenanted by a gentleman and his family

A photograph of Mannsfield taken after the Civil War showing the ravages of war. Mannsfield was used as a hospital after the engagement at Prospect Hill. *Courtesy of the National Park Service.*

who lived in a new home, the grove not far distant. They were people of culture whose ancestors sought and found homes in Virginia. Mrs. S.— now I think dead—was born and raised in Spotsylvania County and was endowed with what is called clairvoyance, a gift known among all people and in all races and times. Walking out into her yard and pointing to a certain chestnut tree, Mrs. S. would ask if you did not see men in uniform under the tree? She could see a doctor ministering to the wounded under another tree, officers with their side arms, all moving to and fro; orderlies holding two or more horses, etc. She could not understand why others could not see what she saw.

Mrs. S. has often told me that she saw men in Confederate uniforms walking back and forth under the trees and seemed annoyed that I could not do so.

Mrs. S. would not be the only tenant of Mannsfield who witnessed the spirits of the past while living around the old ruins. A neighbor identified only as Mrs. Yerby who lived at Hamilton's Crossing reported to William Bernard Sr., that she frequently spotted the ghosts of Confederate soldiers at Mannsfield. Even members of the Bernard family sighted the spectral soldiers. During a visit to Mannsfield, William Bernard Sr.'s mother, Isabella Roberts Bernard, awoke in the middle of the night while staying in the tenant's house to see the ghost of a Confederate officer standing at the foot of the bed. Isabella Bernard was not frightened by her nocturnal visitor. Instead of being spooked, she rolled over in bed and went back to sleep.

The Bernard family sold the property to R.A. James, who proceeded to liquidate Mannsfield remaining assets. In the early 1920s, the remaining sandstone blocks that were used to construct the mansion house of Mannsfield were purchased by artist Gari Melchers, who moved the blocks to build his studio at Belmont in Stafford County. By the 1930s, the remains of the basement were all that stood of the once grand house. Finally, what was left of Mannsfield was bulldozed to make space for I-95. While the physical remains of Mannsfield have been lost to history, the memory of this once grand plantation lives on in the history of Spotsylvania County in part due to the memory of the soldiers, Union and Confederate, who imprinted the land they fought and died for.

10

CHATHAM MANOR

Above the Rappahannock River in Stafford County stands Chatham Manor. Built in 1771, Chatham has witnessed the birth of a nation, the sins of slavery, a bloody civil war and reconstruction. Today, Chatham is part of the National Park Service, where it tells the story of the plantation's role in the Battle of Fredericksburg and its use as a Civil War hospital. Chatham is also known for the Lady in White, Fredericksburg's most notorious ghost. While a great yarn, the legend of the Lady in White obscures the true history of Chatham, which is richer and more complex than any made-up ghost story. The real-life tragedy that occurred at Chatham was not the thwarting of young lovers but the perpetration of chattel slavery.

After three years of construction, planter and statesman William Fitzhugh moved into Chatham Manor with his wife, Ann Bolling Fitzhugh, and their children in 1771. The plantation was named after William Pitt, 1st Earl of Chatham, a British politician who championed the colonial cause before the American Revolution. Chatham was built in the Georgian style by enslaved Black labor. During the construction of Chatham, a notice ran in the *Virginian Gazette* that William Hanover, a "good house carpenter and joiner," had fled from the plantation on September 17, 1769. It is unknown if Hanover was ever captured.

The Fitzhugh family were renowned for their hospitality, and William Fitzhugh's good friend George Washington was a frequent visitor to Chatham. Besides farming, Fitzhugh also had a racetrack constructed on the property for horse racing. It was only through the labor of the enslaved Black men, women and children that William Fitzhugh and his family were able to live in luxury during the colonial period and Revolutionary War. Fitzhugh was clearly proud of his plantation and boasted in an advertisement that his enslaved workers were "for the number as likely and as valuable a set of Negroes as any in Virginia." To Fitzhugh, the people he enslaved were commodities that brought him wealth, not individual people with their own hopes and dreams.

By the 1790s, William Fitzhugh could no longer afford the upkeep of Chatham, and he advertised that the plantation and his enslaved workers were for sale. Fitzhugh placed an advertisement for the property, writing:

> *The subscriber…offers for sale the following Land and Negroes, at prices so reduced as to claim the attention of persons wishing to invest money in such property…about two hundred and thirty Negroes, of different ages, sizes and description. A sale of them by families will be preferred; to effect this they will be offered at a reduced price.*

The riverside entrance of Chatham Manor, built for William Fitzhugh in 1771. According to legend, the ghost of the Lady in White is seen walking the grounds of Chatham every seven years. *Author's photo.*

Fitzhugh and his family moved to Alexandira but left most of his enslaved workers to tend to the property and cultivate the land while he searched for a buyer. In a letter Fitzhugh wrote to a friend, he moaned, "At present I am a slave, nay worse than a slave, for I labour with my Body and my mind in continually harass'd [sic]."

In January 1805, the enslaved field workers rebelled against the overseer, Mr. Starke. The overseer had attempted to end the enslaved workers' Christmas holiday early and demanded that they return to their labors. From the eighteenth to the early part of the nineteenth century, Christmas in Virginia was celebrated from Christmas Day to Twelfth Night. These twelve days were a time when labor for enslaved field workers was suspended, and they were given passes to travel to neighboring plantations to visit family and friends. Extra food and alcohol were given to the enslaved along with new clothing, shoes and blankets. It was a bright time for people whose daily lives were so closely regulated.

Angered by Mr. Starke's demand, the enslaved workers resisted by seizing the overseer and binding him. The enslaved workers then proceeded to whip him. Starke was able to escape and fled to Falmouth, where he enlisted four white men to return to Chatham to subdue the slave revolt. The revolt was subdued, and an enslaved man named Philip was killed. Another enslaved man named James attempted to flee and drowned in the Rappahannock River. Three other enslaved men—Abraham, Robin and Cupid—were seized. Abraham was executed for "conspiracy and insurrection." Initially sentenced to death, Robin and Cupid were sent out of the state. They were likely sent to Louisiana or transported to the Caribbean. Regardless of where they were sent, it was a virtual death sentence, as transported slaves typically did not live long on the brutal rice or sugar plantations. After Abraham's execution and the transportation of Robin and Cupid, William Fitzhugh petitioned the State of Virginia for $1,400 for the lost revenue of his enslaved workers. This request was rejected by the state.

Nine years after placing Chatham Manor for sale, William Fitzhugh sold his 1,280-acre property to Major Churchill Jones for $20,000. A veteran of the Revolutionary War, Jones improved the estate by building the terraces down to the Rappahannock River and constructed the first bridge across the Rappahannock River. Following Major Jones's death, Chatham went to his brother William Jones, a planter who lived at Ellwood in Orange County. William Jones gifted Chatham to his daughter Hannah upon her marriage to Virginia Court of Appeals judge John Coalter. This was Hannah's second marriage. Hannah Jones Coalter lived at Chatham with her husband and her disabled daughter, Janet.

In 1838, Judge John Coalter died, and his widow continued to live at Chatham. Along with caring for her daughter, Hannah Coalter often had her younger half-sister Betty Churchill Jones stay at Chatham for extended visits. In 1848, Betty Churchill Jones married her former tutor James Horace Lacy. The Lacy's inherited Ellwood and stood to eventually acquire Chatham Manor. Before her death, Hannah Coalter attempted to free her ninety-two enslaved workers in her will. However, the laws of Virginia required that all manumitted slaves had to leave Virginia within a year of receiving their freedom. Coalter wrote in her will that her enslaved workers were allowed to choose their next owners, or they could be manumitted with a small endowment to support themselves in a free state or in the African colony of Liberia.

After Hannah Coalter's death in 1857, her executors sued to stop the manumission of her slaves. They argued that enslaved people were legally incapable of choosing whether to remain enslaved or free based on the Dred Scott decision. The local Stafford court agreed that the dictates of Coalter's will should be carried out, but the Virginia Supreme Court disagreed and sided with Coalter's executors. Only Charles, Coalter's household administrator, was freed outright following her death. The executors then sold Chatham and the plantation's enslaved workers to J. Horace Lacy.

Irate with the court's decision, Ellen Mitchell, an enslaved laundress at Chatham, publicly complained that her freedom had been taken away from her by Lacy. To rid himself of Mitchell, Lacy sold her to James Aler, a slave trader in Fredericksburg. Aler allowed Mitchell a ninety-day pass to leave Fredericksburg to raise money to purchase her freedom. Mitchell and one of her sons traveled to Washington, D.C., Baltimore, Philadelphia, New York City, and Boston, where she lectured about her plight and the cruelty of slavery. Mitchell was successful in raising the necessary funds to purchase her and her children's freedom. Lacy also freed Mitchell's mother, and the family moved to Cincinnati, Ohio, where they opened a laundry.

J. Horace Lacy was a vocal proponent of secession and joined the Confederate army as a staff officer. Betty Lacy stayed at Chatham with her children until 1862, when Stafford was occupied by the Union army. The Lacy family would not return to Chatham until after the Civil War. Chatham was used as a headquarters and hospital throughout the remainder of the war. In 1862, President Abraham Lincoln visited Chatham when the plantation was serving as the headquarters of General Irvin McDowell.

Chatham is only one of three houses visited by both George Washington and Abraham Lincoln. The other sites are Mount Vernon and Berkeley Plantation, all in Virginia.

During the Battle of Fredericksburg, Union general Edwin Sumner observed the battle from Chatham while artillery batteries shelled the town from the adjacent bluffs. Following the battle, the wounded were taken to Chatham, where army surgeons performed amputations. Walt Whitman, Clara Barton and Dr. Mary Edwards Walker tended to the wounded at Chatham. In a published account, Whitman remembered noticing outside the house at the foot of a tree "a heap of amputated feet, legs, arms, hands, etc.—about a load for a one-horse cart. Several dead bodies lie near." More than 130 Union soldiers died at Chatham during the war and were buried on the grounds. After the war, the remains were disinterred and moved to the Fredericksburg National Cemetery. In the twentieth century, three graves were discovered and marked with a military headstone. The identities of the three soldiers who remain at Chatham are unknown.

During the winter of 1862–63, the plantation was used as an army camp. Dorothea Dix of the United State Sanitary Commission operated a soup kitchen at Chatham. Soldiers tore the paneling from the house to use as firewood and wrote their names on the walls. In May 1863, Chatham was used as a hospital again following the Battle of Chancellorsville and the Second Battle of Fredericksburg.

In November 1865, the Lacy's returned to Chatham to find the house badly damaged. Unable to maintain the plantation without slave labor or afford the necessary repairs to the building, J. Horace Lacy sold Chatham to a Pennsylvania banker for $23,900. Chatham would go through a succession of owners until Daniel Bradford Devore and his wife, Helen Steward Devore, purchased the property in the 1920s. The Devores began to restore the property and built the large, walled English-style garden. In 1931, the Devores sold Chatham to John Lee Pratt and his wife for $150,000. Pratt was an executive with General Motors, and during World War II, he invited General George Marshall and General Dwight D. Eisenhower to relax and to go duck hunting on the property. The Pratts would be the last private owners of Chatham. Following John Pratt's death in 1975, Chatham Manor was bequeathed to the National Park Service, and the building now serves as the headquarters for the Fredericksburg and Spotsylvania National Military Park.

The legend of the Lady in White has obscured the true history of Chatham Manor and the horrors of slavery. By focusing on the Lady in

A cannon still looms over Fredericksburg from the terrace of Chatham. In December 1862, Union artillery bombarded the city for four hours. *Author's photo.*

White, paranormal researchers have overlooked the documented history of the 1805 Slave Revolt and J. Horace Lacy's role in blocking the emancipation of the enslaved workers in 1857. There was a lot of pain and suffering that occurred at the plantation before Chatham was used as a hospital during the Civil War. All these emotions have been embedded into the ground and the building.

It should not be surprising that over time people have claimed to have witnessed ghosts at Chatham Manor. By the early twentieth century, there were accounts of people witnessing a woman in white at Chatham. The earliest documented account about the Lady in White comes from author Edith Tunis Sale in her book *Manors of Virginia in Colonial Times* published in 1909:

> And when the moon rises back of the woodlands, or only stars light the silent night, back and forth through the dew-drenched hedges trips "the White Lady," silently weeping and wringing her hands. Who she is, or

The tree where poet Walt Whitman witnessed heaps of amputated limbs piled up. *Author's photo.*

why she walks there, no one is able to tell; yet night after night, through century and century, this sad wraith of some once gay being haunts the "Ghost Walk" of Chatham, perhaps in heart broken [sic] longing for the days forever irrecoverable.

During the early part of the twentieth century, ghost stories in Virginia were used by owners of properties as evidence as to why the sites were historically important and that the sites deserved to be restored. The owners of Chatham used the sightings of a Lady in White to connect the plantation to its historic past. The legend of the Lady in White connected the house to the romantic days of the colonial period. Instead of focusing on Chatham's dark history, the Lady in White became a romantic figure of a bygone day when colonial dames and squires spent their days in luxury and were entertained by the jolly William Fitzhugh.

Paranormal researcher Marguerite DuPont Lee solidified the legend of the Lady in White in her book *Virginia Ghosts*. Lee was born in Wilmington, Delaware, in 1862 to Eleuthere Irénée DuPont and Charlotte Henderson.

Eleuthere DuPont was the manager of the DuPont powder mill. Her mother, Charlotte Henderson, was born in Virginia and was the daughter of Archibald Henderson, the commandant of the Marine Corps. In 1877, Lee was orphaned and was raised by her older sister. At the age of eighteen, she married her cousin Cazenove Gardner Lee, a successful lawyer, and moved to Washington, D.C. With her husband, Lee had two sons: Cazenove Gardner Lee Jr. and Maurice DuPont Lee. While living in Washington, D.C., Lee spent the humid summers at Menokin, the Lee family estate. Her husband died in 1912, when Lee was fifty years old. Following her husband's death, she built and managed a tenement in Georgetown. Lee was also a suffragist and participated in the 1913 Woman's Suffrage Procession in Washington, D.C.

After living at the Georgetown Settlement for several years, Marguerite DuPont Lee gave the tenement to the Salvation Army and moved to a suite at the Powhatan Hotel. During her retirement, Lee continued her charitable endeavors and devoted her time to paranormal research. "She was Virginian enough to know that the stories were largely legendary, but at the same time, she was prepared to believe that underlying them, there was some genuine, inexplicable psychic manifestation," Ludwell

The grave of an unknown Union soldier who was buried at Chatham Manor. During the Civil War, 130 Union soldiers were buried at Chatham. *Author's photo.*

Lee Montague wrote in his 1966 introduction of Lee's book. Because she was part of the Virginian elite, Lee was able to visit the grand homes of the gentry and interview the owners about their ghost stories. Marguerite DuPont Lee died in 1936 and is buried in the Congressional Cemetery in Washington, D.C.

In *Virginia Ghosts*, Marguerite DuPont Lee passed on this legend of the Lady in White. According to Lee:

> *The late Mrs. Randolph Howard, for a short time Chatham's gracious hostess, related to friends that on several occasions she had seen the White Lady in the garden walking up and down a path, leading by way of some marble steps on the terrace below, known as the "Ghost Walk." The White Lady is reputedly always seen once in seven years, on the 21st of June, between noon and midnight. Mrs. Howard saw her in the afternoon. She had no idea of her ghost's name or history and seldom spoke freely on the subject, fearing the servants would be frightened.*

Mrs. Howard claimed that she had a friend who was a scholar who was in Newark, New Jersey, when she found a book written in French that detailed the identity of the Lady in White of Chatham. The author had stayed at Chatham in the nineteenth century and was told that during the colonial era an Englishman and his beautiful daughter came to visit William Fitzhugh. The Englishman, who was a celebrated man of letters, had brought his daughter to Virginia to find her a suitable husband after she had fallen in love with a poor drysalter in London. According to the legend, the daughter had met the tradesman after her beloved pet parrot died and she visited his establishment to have her pet preserved. The couple fell madly in love and planned to elope. Her father found out about the planned elopement and whisked her off to Virginia.

The Englishman was a friend of Ann Fitzhugh and was invited for an extended visit to Chatham. Despite being warmly entertained by William and Ann Fitzhugh, the daughter was miserable and missed her lover. Unbeknownst to the young woman, her lover had followed her to Virginia. After finding his love at Chatham, the gallant lover was able to pass letters to her through the young woman's maid. They again planned another elopement. The lover had procured a rope ladder he would throw up to her window. A boat moored on the Rappahannock River would be waiting for the couple. Somehow the woman's father found out about the plan and locked his daughter in her room at Chatham every night.

While this drama was going on, George Washington was also visiting his good friend William Fitzhugh at Chatham. Washington's valet, Billy Lee, overheard the drysalter's plan to rescue his love and told his enslaver what he had found out. Being an honorable man, Washington went to the woman's father, and they devised a plan. On the night that the elopement was to happen, Washington and Billy Lee caught the lover and had him locked up in a shed. Washington then went to the woman's window with a rope ladder, and when she climbed down, she was caught by the future father of his country and was taken back to her father. Enraged, the father took his daughter back to England, where he quickly arranged a marriage for her with a suitable man. Despite having ten children with her husband, the woman never forgot her first love. "On her death-bed [*sic*] she announced her intention of walking in Spirit on the anniversary of her death, in the Lady's Walk on the terrace at Chatham, a favorite spot with her. She died June 21, 1790," Lee wrote.

Mrs. Howard lived at Chatham from 1909 to 1914—she was the one who created the legend of the Lady in White. There is no corroborating evidence to support the story of an elopement at Chatham. George Washington had one of the most documented lives in American history, and it was not until the twentieth century was there any mention of his involvement in stopping an elopement. Mrs. Howard likely invented the story to highlight Chatham's historic past and make it stand out amid a sea of historic haunted plantations vying for visitors. It is possible that Mrs. Howard saw a ghostly white figure while living at Chatham and decided to create the backstory. The first account of the Lady in White in 1909 stated that at that time the identity of the Lady in White was unknown. In ghost stories, the unknown woman in white (or gray, brown and so on) is a popular trope. The romantic backstory adds to the allure.

The Lady in White is supposed to return every seven years, but she has been a no-show since the National Park Service acquired Chatham in 1976. In 1986, several Park Service rangers held a vigil for the Lady in White; sadly, they saw nothing that night. Though the Lady in White has not made an appearance in decades, guests have reported seeing strange things at Chatham. People in nineteenth-century clothing have been seen on the property. Only recently, an acquittance told me that while visiting Chatham Manor she saw a Civil War nurse walking down the hall of the plantation. This is not the only Civil War era ghost seen on the property. One day, a Civil War reenactor arrived early for a scheduled living history program. While unloading his gear, he saw a contingent of men in Union uniforms.

But on returning to his car, the soldiers had disappeared, and he was alone at the site. In Fredericksburg, residents who live in the houses facing the Rappahannock River have claimed that at dawn and dusk they have seen cannons lining the bluffs with sentries standing guard.

If there is a Lady in White haunting the grounds of Chatham, I believe that she could be the distressed spirit of Hannah Jones Coalter, whose final wishes were disregarded by the greed of J. Hoarce and Betty Lacy. Perhaps she is still walking the grounds so that we can remember the injustice that occurred to the enslaved Black men, women and children she tried to free. Through ghost stories, we can learn about the past, but only if we tell the true story of what really occurred at the site. I hope that whoever the Lady in White may be that she has found peace and that we don't forget the dark history of Chatham. Only through remembrance can we make the future a better place.

11

AQUIA EPISCOPAL CHURCH

The beautiful and historic Aquia Episcopal Church has been the heart of the community since 1667. Located in Stafford County, in Overwharton Parish, Aquia Church is the oldest established church in the county. Today, visitors and congregants continue to gather to worship in the historic structure, which dates to the 1750s. Aquia Church has a fascinating history: it witnessed the birth of the nation and the destruction of the Civil War. Naturally, such a historic structure has also acquired a few ghostly tales.

In 1667, Aquia Church was established to serve the spiritual needs of Overwharton Parish. During the colonial period, the Anglican Church was the official religion of the Virginia colony. Virginians were required to attend services at their local parish church at least once a month and were taxed by the parish to pay the for clergy, maintain the parish church and provide for the poor and indigent. Aquia Church took its name from nearby Aquia Creek and was placed off the main road (now Telegraph Road) of Stafford County, allowing for easy access to the site.

The original structure was a simple wooden chapel, but by the mid-1700s, the parish had decided that a new, finer structure was needed. Construction of the church began in 1751 and continued until 1755, when disaster struck. As reported in the *Virginia Gazette* on March 21, 1755:

> *We hear from Stafford County, that the new Church at Aquia, one of the best Building in the Colony (and the old wooden one near it) were burnt*

down on the 17th Instant, by the carelessness of some of the Carpenters leaving Fire too near the Shavings, at Night, when they left off Work. This fine Building was within two or three Days Work of being compleatly [sic] finished and delivered up by the Undertakers.

The church was quickly rebuilt, and in 1757, the structure was completed. With its Flemish bond brickwork of Aquia sandstone from the local quarry on Government Island, the structure is an elegant building.

The church also has a beautiful and historic cemetery. In Virginia, all parish churches were to have a cemetery on the grounds. Church cemeteries in the colonial period were for those who did not have a family cemetery to be buried in. Until the mid-nineteenth century, those who were buried in a church cemetery were people who lived in towns or cities, the middle class,

Aquia Episcopal Church in Stafford County was constructed in 1757. According to legend, the church is haunted by the ghost of a beautiful woman who was murdered in the church after the Revolutionary War. *Author's photo.*

travelers who died away from their family home and the poor. Most wealthy or gentry families who owned plantations or large farms had enough land to lay out a family cemetery on their own property. To have enough land to set aside for a burial ground was a sign of wealth. Occasionally, members of the gentry chose to be buried in their parish church cemetery if they lived close enough to the church to easily transport the body to the cemetery or if they were high-ranking members of the church such as clergy or had served on the church vestry.

The cemetery in Aquia Church has some of the finest examples of eighteenth-century gravestones in Virginia. Because of the expense, southern gravestones in the seventeenth and eighteenth centuries tended to be more sedate than the ones seen in the northern colonies. Also, many early gravestones did not survive the ravages of the Civil War. Despite some damage to the Aquia Church Cemetery during the Civil War, there are some stunning examples of early American funereal art. On the gravestone of Christian Graham, her grieving husband paid for grim skull and crossbones to decorate the head of the grave. Under the eyeless sockets of the skull, the words *Memento Mori* are carved on a flowing ribbon. Inscribed on the grave is the following:

> *Here lies the Body of CHRISTIAN the wife of JOHN GRAHAM Merch* [merchant] *and daughter of Doctor GUSTAVUS BROWN She departed this Life the 17 of September 1742 in the 23 Year of her Ag* [age] *when she had been married not quite 2 Months There was no Person more universally esteem nor sincerely lamented by her acquaintance.*

Nearby the grave of Christian Graham are two tabletop graves where the family of the deceased added the family crest and cherubs. Sadly, these markers have been severely weathered by time and the inscriptions are unreadable.

Strange things have also been witnessed in the Aquia Church Cemetery. Paranormal researcher L.B. Taylor interviewed Robert Frazier, who had been the caretaker for several years. Frazier admitted to seeing an apparition in the cemetery. According to Frazier, they were "blurred and funny." The apparition was seen only at night and was white in color and solid. Frazier's son, who assisted him, also saw the apparitions, yet when they went to investigate, the figures disappeared.

Aquia Church withstood the turmoil of the American Revolution and the establishment of the Episcopal Church in the United States. The Episcopal

The grave of Christian Graham features a stunning Memento Mori, an unusual feature on a Virginian gravestone. *Author's photo.*

Church replaced the Anglican Church in the United States; the new Episcopal Church was based in the new nation and no longer followed the dictates of the Church of England. Following the war, church membership in the Episcopal Church declined in Virginia due to the Virginia Statute for Religious Freedom, which was enacted in 1786. The Statute for Religious Freedom allowed Virginians to worship at any congregation that they wished to and abolished the parish tax that supported the Anglican Church.

For the first half of the nineteenth century, Aquia Church struggled to attract new members, as the Methodist and Presbyterian Churches became the dominant denominations in the area. By the 1850s, things had begun to look brighter as a new rector brought life back to the old church. The rebirth of Aquia Church was threatened by the Civil War. Aquia Church was occupied by both Confederate and Union soldiers between 1861 and 1865. The structure was protected during the Union occupation by army chaplain Reverend Henry Wheeler, who used Aquia Church to hold religious services for Union soldiers.

Despite the best efforts of Reverend Wheeler, the war left its toll on Aquia Church. Solider graffiti from both sides were etched on the church walls, windows were missing, pews had been chewed on by cavalry horses and gravestones in the church cemetery had been disinterred to build fireplaces. Unlike many rural churches damaged by the Civil War, Aquia Church was restored to its former glory and continues to serve the spiritual needs of Stafford County.

With such a rich and colorful history, it is to be expected that the site has a few ghostly legends attached to it. In the 1930s, paranormal researcher Marguerite DuPont Lee visited Aquia Church and interviewed parishioners about the church's ghosts. The story they related sounded like a tale ripped from a gothic novel. According to legend, following the Revolutionary War, when the church was abandoned, a beautiful young woman was murdered in the church by two highwaymen and her body was hidden in the belfry. The highwaymen expected their crime to remain hidden, but when parishioners returned to Aquia Church in the early 1800s, they discovered a bloodstain on a flagstone. Further investigation uncovered the skeletal remains of a young woman with beautiful blonde hair still attached to her skull. Out of pity for the unknown woman, the parishioners buried her in an unmarked grave in the church cemetery. It was said that the bloody flagstone stood as mute testimony of the woman's murder until the flagstone was removed during church renovations. Though she may have received a proper burial, the restless spirit of the murdered woman wanders the church at midnight seeking justice from beyond the grave.

The story became ingrained in the community to such an extent that according to Lee, "under no circumstances could any man in Stafford County be induced to enter the church at night." It should be noted that there is no evidence in the historic record to corroborate the legend of the murdered woman. Regardless of the lack of corroboration, many in Stafford County believed that there was a ghost at Aquia Church. "Everyone speaks of sounds in the church as though someone was running up and down stairs. A number of people have heard heavy noises, suggesting a struggle was taking place. Upon entering—all is quiet," local resident Agnes Moncure recounted to Lee.

One legend about Aquia Church claimed that a would-be ghost hunter was actually scared to death after he accepted a dare to climb the belfry after dark. The man was to climb the belfry at midnight. To prove to his friends that he had completed his daring feat, he was to hammer a nail into the belfry wall. Thus, equipped with a hammer and nail, the young trespasser entered the church and climbed the belfry. But in the dark, the man, proving that he was not the town genius, accidentally nailed his coat to the wall. When he attempted to enact his escape after committing vandalism, he found that he could not move, as something was holding his coat in place. Rather than pull himself loose, the man was said to have died of freight, thus committing a favor to the community that he was not able to pass on his genes to the next generation. Of course, this has the hallmark of legend, as a similar story is told about several haunted locations around the world.

Another story told to Lee that may have a basis in fact regarded a wealthy resident of Stafford who was fascinated by ghost stories and haunted locations. Finding that none of the local men would join her in an overnight investigation at Aquia Church, she invited two scientists from Washington, D.C., for a paranormal investigation. Upon entering the church, the woman was slapped across the face by an unseen hand. The scientists could not reach a possible explanation for what had happened.

The exterior of Aquia Episcopal Church is covered with graffiti left behind by Civil War soldiers from both sides. *Author's photo.*

The interior of Aquia Episcopal Church. During the Civil War, two Confederates were saved from being captured by Union troops when they were awakened by a whistling ghost. *Author's photo.*

Despite the slapping, Lee uncovered a story that suggested that the ghost of Aquia Church was a helpful spirit. During the Civil War, two young Confederate soldiers, William Fitzhugh and an unidentified companion, decided to spend the night at Aquia Church after spending the day scouting the terrain. The young men decided to make their beds in the church pews, but their rest was disturbed by the sounds of footsteps at the rear of the church on the stone flagging. Then Fitzhugh and his friend heard the tune "The Campbells Are Coming" being whistled. The whistling and footsteps drew closer to the soldiers. Upon the approach of the footsteps, Fitzhugh and his friend struck a light to reveal that they were alone. Unnerved by the sounds, Fitzhugh decided to check the church door to ensure that it was locked when they spotted Union soldiers approaching. The young Confederates had just enough time to jump out of a window. According to Lee, for the remainder of his life, Fitzhugh "always attributed their escape to the whistling of the ghost." Due to the friendly ghost, Fitzhugh and his companion were able to escape the church in the nick of time.

Despite the lurid legend behind the church, the spirit that haunts the Aquia Church appears to be a benevolent one. Aquia Church is open to the public as a historic landmark and as an active church. Visitors are welcome to attend worship services or to arrange a tour of the church.

12

SPOTSYLVANIA CONFEDERATE CEMETERY

The Civil War completely ravaged Virginia. The war destroyed farmland and robbed families of their young men. With the Confederate capital located in Richmond approximately sixty miles to the south and the Union capital in Washington, D.C., located approximately sixty miles to the north, Spotsylvania County became the crossroads of the Civil War. Between 1862 and 1864, four major battles—Fredericksburg, Chancellorsville, Wilderness and Spotsylvania Courthouse—were fought in or around the region, and countless soldiers on both sides camped and marched through Spotsylvania County.

The battle of Spotsylvania Court House, which occurred from May 8 to 21, 1864, hit the county the hardest. Following the Battle of the Wilderness, which had ended in a Union defeat, instead of pulling his troops back across the Rappahannock River, Lieutenant General Ulysses S. Grant issued orders that the Army of the Potomac would move toward Spotsylvania Court House. Grant hoped to capture Richmond and cripple General Robert E. Lee's Army of the Potomac. "Wherever Lee goes, there you will go also," Grant told Major General George Meade. Believing that Spotsylvania could be easily captured, Major General Gouverneur K. Warren's forces stumbled upon the Confederate army and the battle began. On the first day of fighting, May 8, 1864, Major General John Sedgwick was killed by a Confederate sharpshooter. Sedgwick was the highest-ranking Union officer killed during the Civil War. Spotsylvania Court House turned into a brutal deadlock. To protect their position, the Army of Northern Virginia established a long line of earthworks.

On May 12, 1864, Grant moved his forces against a half-mile bulge in the earthworks called the Mule Shoe Salient. Amid a torrential downpour, Union and Confederate soldiers fought in brutal combat for twenty-two hours. After the battle, this section of land becomes known as the Bloody Angle. The Bloody Angle claimed 17,000 casualties. Despite the Union soldiers forcing the Confederates from their earthworks, the Confederates were able to fall back and create a new line of earthworks. Exhausted from fighting, the Union army was unable to press the advantage. Grant resumed fighting on May 18, 1864, but the Union was easily repulsed by artillery fire. After twelve days of fighting, both sides pulled out of their defenses. Although the outcome of the battle was inconclusive, both sides claimed Spotsylvania Court House as a victory. The war would continue for another bloody year. The estimated number of casualties from the inconclusive Battle of Spotsylvania Court House was 31,086 soldiers killed, wounded and missing.

Confederate dead following the Battle of Spotsylvania Court House in 1864. Following the war, the Confederate dead were moved to the Spotsylvania Confederate Cemetery. *Courtesy of Library of Congress, LC-DIG-ppmsca-32912.*

When the smoke of battle cleared, hundreds of Southern soldiers lay dead far from homes and a decent burial. During the Civil War, it was left to the victor of a battle or engagement to bury the dead of both sides. Naturally, the winning side would take greater care burying their comrades than the men who had tried to kill them. Following the Confederate withdrawal at the Mule Shoe Salient on May 13, 1864, the Union soldiers who secured the earthworks buried the dead, Union and Confederate, in the trenches that had been dug by their foes. The survivors tossed the dead down into the trenches and kicked dirt from the adjacent parapet to cover the dead. "The unfortunate victims [had] unwittingly dug their own grave," a Union soldier wrote.

While the Confederates were left in unmarked graves, the Union soldiers took great care to carefully mark and record the burial sites of their friends and comrades. These records were used after the war when the federal government sent the First Veteran Volunteers to Spotsylvania to locate and rebury the Union dead in June 1865. The recovered remains of the Union dead found in Spotsylvania were then transported to Fredericksburg, where they joined their fallen comrades from the Battles of Fredericksburg, Chancellorsville, and the Wilderness. Though the First Veteran Volunteers were ordered to bury only Union dead, the veteran soldiers disobeyed their orders and buried any Confederates they found.

Into this void, Southern women stepped in, as they could not abide their sons and loved ones being forgotten and lying in unmarked graves. Throughout the South, women formed Ladies Memorial Associations (LMA). The purpose of the LMA was to locate and transport the Confederate dead to specially created cemeteries. Like the federal cemeteries, the LMAs purchased land, frequently on or near the battlefields where the soldiers had fallen. In 1866, the Spotsylvania Chapter of the LMA was formed to care for the Spotsylvania Confederate dead. Because it was difficult to transport the dead to Fredericksburg, the ladies of Spotsylvania purchased five acres of land for the Spotsylvania Confederate Cemetery. Maintained by the Spotsylvania Memorial Association, nearly six hundred Confederate soldiers were reburied in the cemetery. Grouped by state, the soldiers rest with their comrades in neat rows. Unlike the headstones of Union soldiers, which have rounded tops, the headstones for Confederate soldiers are topped with a point. In the center of the cemetery is a granite shaft with a stone Confederate soldier atop the memorial—a silent guard over his fallen comrades. The cemetery is a tranquil place.

I first visited the cemetery in May 2014. It was the 150th anniversary of the Battle of Spotsylvania Courthouse. As part of the anniversary ceremonies and historical reenactment of the battle, an illumination of the cemetery was organized. A small candle was placed in a luminaria and lit at each grave. As I wandered through the cemetery at dusk, I was struck by the sheer number of graves. Boys from Alabama, Arkansas, Georgia, Louisiana, Missouri, North Carolina, South Carolina, Tennessee, Texas and Virginia surrounded me on all sides. But what really captured my interest was the section devoted to the unknown soldiers. Over two hundred soldiers were buried with no identification—their families were left to wonder about their fates and final burial place.

While walking through the rows of graves, I began to smell the pungent aroma of cigar smoke. Looking around, I realized that no one was close by. A group of Confederate reenactors was off in another section at the far end of the cemetery, but none of them were smoking. I called my mom over to smell the aroma, and she confirmed that I was indeed smelling cigar smoke. I moved on, continuing my walk through the section of unknowns. A few minutes later, I stopped again and sniffed the air. I instantly recognized the scent as cigar smoke. Having smelled phantom cigar smoke several times while working at the Whaley House in San Diego, California, I was able to recognize the smell. The scent seemed to come and go as if the smoker was slowly ambling along with us. Because I had attended the reenactment of the battle that had taken place earlier in the day, I was in period attire. Perhaps the spirit of a fallen Confederate was attracted to me because I was wearing the fashions of his day.

I could smell the scent for as long as I stayed in the unknown section. My mom could also detect the cigar smoke as we moved along. As an experiment, I moved over to another section to see if the scent would follow. When I did move to the section next to the unknown section, I could no longer smell the cigar smoke. But on my return to the unknown section, I was greeted by the distinct odor of cigar smoke. I received the impression that there was a Confederate soldier who had been attracted by the illumination and had made his presence known to show his appreciation to the tribute being paid to him and his comrades. It was a memorable and moving experience; for one moment I had connected with a long-lost soldier who calls Virginia his final home.

13

BARNES & NOBLE

The Barnes & Noble in the Central Park Shopping Center at 1220 Carl D Silver Pkwy is one of my favorite places in Fredericksburg. I am there so frequently that I'm known by the staff. Besides having the best horror section in the area, the bookshop is also haunted. At first glance, the building appears to be an odd choice to be haunted, as the building is of modern construction. But anyone familiar with paranormal activity knows that the age of the structure is immaterial to a haunting. It is the land and what happened on the site that in many cases tie to the haunting.

Before the building that houses Barnes & Noble was constructed, the area was made up of small family farms. Over time, these farms were bought up, and modern shopping structures were built to service the growing communities of Fredericksburg, Stafford, Spotsylvania and Caroline Counties. The land has seen hundreds of years of history from Indigenous peoples and the colonial era to the Civil War. It appears that something from the land and the people who lived and worked on it remains today.

Not long after Barnes & Noble opened, it became apparent to the staff that the building was haunted. In the morning, when staff entered the building to open the store, they would hear the voice of a woman saying, "Good morning." Frequently they would hear their name being called when they were the only person in the building. Jane, the head book buyer, experienced this so many times that they started to call the woman the Borders Ghost after the store that was in the building previously.

Seeking more answers to the identity of the Borders Ghost, Jane allowed paranormal author and investigator Pamela K. Kinney to investigate.

The Barnes & Noble in Central Park is haunted by the ghosts of a man and a woman who like to greet the staff. *Author's photo*.

Kinney graciously shared with me the results of her investigation, which uncovered more than one ghost in the bookstore. Through a ghost box, Kinney was able to communicate with the spirit of a man who answered in the affirmative when asked if anyone was present. Kinney tried to determine what period the man was from, asking if he was from the Revolutionary War, the War of 1812 or the Civil War. The man did not answer, so perhaps he was from a different era than the ones mentioned. After this line of questioning, Kinney asked if the man was haunting the bookstore. Again, there was no answer. But when Kinney asked if he was haunting the entire shopping center, a male voice was heard saying, "Yes."

Pamela Kinney then asked the man if he was the one who had spoken to Jane. This question received no response from the man. Jane then said, "I heard you talked to B——. Said good morning to her." To this statement, the man answered "Yes" and then said the name of the staff member. Kinney asked the man if he knew that it was a bookstore, to which the man again said, "Yes." These answers confirmed that the ghost haunting Barnes & Noble was an intelligent spirit.

Kinney concluded the ghost box session and began to investigate other sections of the store. In the children's section, which is in the back of the store near the restrooms, Kinney and Jane stopped to investigate. Upon arriving in the children's section, Kinney noticed a cold spot. This was not caused by an air vent, as the spot was icy cold. Kinney turned on her ghost box and asked, "Are you around me since it's so cold?" To this question, they heard the man's voice say "Yeah!" Then the man said, "Thank you." Kinney then asked for the man's name and if there was more than one spirit present. To the first part of the question, Kinney did not receive an answer, but to the second part, a female answered, "Yes." Following this answer, Kinney asked how many spirits were present. The spirit answered that there were two ghosts in the bookstore. Kinney stated that it sounded as if both the man and the woman answered the question in tandem. She then asked again for a name, to which she heard the name Billy. "You said Billy?" Kinney demanded. "Yes," the man answered. After this answer, the cold spot in the children's section dissipated.

The Fredericksburg Barnes & Noble stocks more than just literary ghosts. Among the works of Edgar Allan Poe, Darcy Coates and Stephen King, the friendly spirits of Billy and the Borders Ghost roam the aisles. Stop by to browse the latest releases and find your next favorite book. Perhaps, if you are lucky, you might even have an interaction with the friendly ghosts that call Barnes & Noble their home.

14

UFO SIGHTINGS

U FOs, or as they are now labeled, UAPs (unidentified anomalous phenomenon), have been in the news lately. Government agencies revealed that they have been investigating UFO sightings for decades, despite maintaining to the public that there was nothing to the phenomenon. Despite pronouncements that UFO disclosure would lead to the collapse of society, each new revelation is greeted by the public with barely a ripple. The Fredericksburg region has had its fair share of UFO sightings, as detailed in this chapter.

Despite it being a well-populated area, there are still areas where sky gazers can revel in the beauty of the night sky away from light pollution. For the aviation enthusiast, the skies above Fredericksburg, Stafford and Spotsylvania host the latest military aircraft from Marine Corps Base Quantico, which lies on the border of Stafford County and Fort Walker (formerly Fort A.P. Hill) in neighboring Caroline County. It is not uncommon to have the peace of Fredericksburg disturbed by the faint rumbles from either site conducting ordnance training. As UFO investigators have noted, there are higher than normal UFO sightings around military installations. I leave it up to the reader to judge if these sightings are from curious extraterrestrial visitors or from the military trying out the latest innovation in military aircraft. Being so close to these military installations, the region's residents are used to seeing strange craft, which makes the following reports even more intriguing. As you shall see, many of the witnesses reiterated in their reports that they are familiar with civilian and military aircraft and that they are not subject to flights of fancy.

Here follows just a sampling of some of the many UFO sighting reports from Fredericksburg, Stafford and Spotsylvania that have been submitted to the National UFO Reporting Center (NUFORC). These reports were compiled by the NUFORC and published on their website database. In most cases, the witness wished to remain anonymous. They just wanted to tell their story without being judged. Regardless of what these witnesses saw, it left a profound effect on them that they were willing to expose themselves to doubt and ridicule by sharing their stories, even in an anonymous database. In some cases, I have edited the statements for clarity, punctuation and grammar.

FREDERICKSBURG

March 18, 2011

Left a friend's house to walk to another residence about a mile down the way, the sky was littered with thunderclouds as earlier [in] *the day it* [had] *stormed heavily, the storm itself was slowly shifting with the winds as if it was preparing itself for another rain. About 60 yards from the house we left, 4 of us in total, noticed a formation of lights and at first just figured it was a passing plane. However, we then noticed it was flying beneath the storm and at a very slow speed, as if it was gliding, and the closer we walked we also noticed no sound. Talking to each other, we joked about how the object is an alien and a friend then blurted out, "Don't judge me." As if on cue, the object actually stopped, which caused the 4 of us to stop and watch, the object then shot out* [a] *beam of light that moved at least 90', you could see the light actually reflecting the clouds, the beam shot upwards then went off. Right after the object then shot itself upwards at unknown speeds, fast enough to have myself and 3 others basically shit our pants. From what it seemed, the object was hiding between the clouds for as we stood there trying to recollect what just occurred, a passenger plane then flew by above the storm, this time its engines clearly audible for a group of people enjoying a walk in the sleeping suburbs of Fredericksburg.*

July 23, 2011

My wife and I heard what sounded like a sonic boom. Seconds later, we saw a very large craft that was traveling in a straight-line northeast toward Washington, D.C.

It was faster than a conventional airliner, but not as fast as a jet fighter. It was white but had a silver belly. It looked just like a C-130, BUT clearly DID NOT have wings!

Like a C-130, the fuselage was wide, and appeared to ramp to the rear, but there were no tail fins. On the belly were two dark grey circles side by side, easily seen as they contrasted from the silver belly. There were two large cylindrical shapes, one on each side as if there was a jet engine mounted directly to the fuselage on each side.

We could see the craft very clearly. We did not see windows, not even in the front cockpit area. There were no markings anywhere. No contrails.

My first thought was that it looked man-made, but we saw it from the side and as it was flying away at an angle. We are convinced that there [was] absolutely no wings on this enormous aircraft.

Unfortunately, we were in a pool, so we did not have a camera. However, I could draw it or give a very accurate description to an artist.

December 9, 2016

Driving on River Rd saw a huge chrome sphere. There were no clouds and [the] sun was reflecting off the object so bright it was blinding. My view of the sky was unblocked 240°. When I first saw it, my first thought was I [had] never seen anything like it before. Then I realized it was hovering. I looked away for 2 seconds and looked back and it was gone out of sight, not possible.

February 9, 2017

Saucer like object with strobing lights and lighted figures seen roaming within Fredericksburg Forest trail.

I was awakened by a loud sound at approx. 3:15 in the morning. The sound appeared hollow and metallic in nature. It sounded as if air was being blown through a large hollow tube.

I ran to look out my window in the direction of the sound. My window faces the forest. I was shocked to see an illuminated rectangular shaped object; the top area of this standing rectangular object was arched (almost like a boxed shape of a man). It moved amongst the trees and from time to time the light would go out. I watched in amazement for what seemed like 3 minutes. There was also another object about 20' away from this object. It was saucer-shaped and had 3 strobing lights around it. It appeared to hover about 15' from the ground. I wanted to capture the images of what I was seeing so I ran and got my cell phone and began recording what I saw.

I recorded the 2 objects and the sound that I heard that woke me up. My footage is 1 minute 23 seconds long. I stopped recording when the saucer like object flew off in the distance.

October 6, 2017

10 triangular disks with blinking lights, solid bright lights, hovering in place then taking off.

More than 10 triangular disk like objects flying low and blinking red and white lights. Often giving off a brighter light for a long period of time, and then blinking. A brighter white light appeared masking the entire shape of one of the saucers. Two of them were hovering in place momentarily before taking off in the same direction followed by eight more. This was on Courthouse Road and Levels Road.

January 24, 2019

While driving west at night, on Rt. 3, about five miles east of Fredericksburg, Virginia, I watched two blue-green light-emitting spheres, flying fast, in tight formation, about 600 feet above the ground, from the southwest toward the northeast. The blue-green lights were unusual and quite beautiful and reminded me a little of lava lamps. They were followed immediately by a pursuing aircraft with familiar, man-made looking navigation lights. This all took about four seconds. I never heard a sound from any of the light's sources.

November 26, 2020

I was out in my backyard walking the dog around 8:00 pm. The moon is bright and it's a clear night, I can see the stars very well. I'm looking up and notice these solid white lights. They seem to circle some stars and then they stay still. Kinda like if they notice me looking at them. There's not just one of these solid lights, sometimes they move in groups of two or more. They change directions very [quickly]. *I thought I was seeing things, so I went* [into] *the house, and I grabbed a flashlight. I flashed it at the night sky. Probably 5 or 6 times. Next thing that happened was amazing and scary at the same time.* [The] *only way I can explain it. Was about 15/20ft from me and about 15ft high was an orange circle, something shot out of it* [which] *looked like a big bright light of energy that was orange and very beautiful, odd shape and shot back into some type of circle. This* [happened] *so fast. If I* [blinked] *my eyes it would have been gone. I've never seen anything like this. Very amazing. I work full time* [and] *been there 15 plus yrs.*

February 9, 2021

My children and I were looking out into the night sky from our front door, when we noticed a large flying craft. It had an orange light/glow and was flying unlike any aircraft that we know of. It would mostly fly upwards, sometimes sideways, and seemed a little jerky or erratic. It also had a beam of light coming down from it. It seemed to be searching for something. It made no sounds like how planes, helicopters, or drones make. The entire time it made no noise and was completely silent. Then after about a minute, it started to dematerialize slowly until it vanished completely while we watched. The night before, my daughter had been playing with a laser pointer and shining it into the sky.

August 2, 2022

My daughter, son in law, and myself were sitting outside and we saw a glowing green neon light, [the] top half looked like an egg and the bottom half was flat, hovering for about 45 seconds. It moved to the left at lightning speed, about a half a mile in less than a second and then stopped and hovered again for about 30 seconds. It then dropped in midair about 150 feet to its original spot. It hovered again for less than a minute and took off at lightning speed back to the right where I originally saw it. I pulled my camera out and it disappeared. There [were] no lights blinking and there was no sound.

March 26, 2023

I was in the back yard doing some astrophotography work and I looked up to see a form flying in a straight path over my house from the east to the west. I couldn't tell what my eyes were seeing exactly and there are two ways to describe it. It looked as though it was a translucent boomerang shape with the curved part as the leading edge. But it also could have been the leading edge of a circular shaped craft with some kind of cloaking device on as the leading-edge shape had a rippling/rippled effect along the translucent appearance. It made no sound and with that and no reference point I could not tell if it was a large object 400-500 feet in the air or a small object 50-60 feet off the ground. The copse of trees and it flew over average 50-80 feet high, so it was at least above that. The air was still. Barely a slight breeze, super clear night, 51 degrees F and cooling off. 95% of all flight paths in my area are N/S coming in and out of Reagan, Dulles, and BWI. I've seen UFO's before, and this one was very unusual as it was very movie like in its quality.

STAFFORD COUNTY

October 31, 2003

On Halloween night 2003, the night was clear when a huge rectangular object flew over my house.

It was Halloween night, October 31, 2003, in Stafford, VA. I was listening to the news [that] evening and heard [that] the International Space Station was to be orbiting over the area and [would] be visible.

Around 1800 hours, I was getting my kids ready for Trick or Treating in the neighborhood. They left around 1810 hours with my wife while I got the bucket filled with candy. I was outside setting up for 2 reasons: 1. So I was comfortable while giving out candy to all the kids. 2. To see if I could get a glimpse of the International Space Station.

At close to 1830 hours, I saw my neighbor across the street on his deck and then immediately a huge rectangular, metallic looking object flew directly over mine and my neighbor's house. We looked at each other and I yelled to him that it was the International Space Station. I also said that I was overwhelmed that they would actually fly the station this close to earth, because it appeared to fly so much lower than what an airplane flies.

I quickly went about the night and [told] everyone I saw the International Space Station. Another neighbor when he and his kids came by was excited to hear what I saw. He asked me to come over to his house the next night because he knew the Station would again be flying over the area the following night.

When I went over to his house the following night, he had his Telescope set up in his backyard. I [was] kidding around with him, telling him he didn't need the telescope because what I saw flew so low, it was clearly visible. He explained that the Station while flying over, you still needed either a Telescope or Binoculars to see it. I then kept my mouth shut and when the station did fly over, what I saw through the Telescope was clearly what I [had] not [seen] the night before.

What I saw [on] Halloween night was rectangular and appeared to be about 50 yards in length. It was metallic, made absolutely no noise, and it flew off so quickly at the time my mind could not comprehend. More specifically, at the moment it passed over, I cognitively thought I was seeing the International Space Station, and with it in space I knew its orbit would pass quickly and what I did not calculate in my mind was the close proximity it was.

The UFO that I saw was not smooth and had its metal fabric skinned over even fitting it precisely. What I'm saying is the skin had nooks and crevices. There were no lights but appeared to have been laminated from the reflective lights of our neighborhood. I only had 2 seconds to see and comprehend what I saw, because [of how] *fast, as it appeared it too had disappeared.*

August 29, 2007

Terrestrials sighted close to Quantico Military Base.

I just let my two dogs out in the backyard and the older female started going crazy as she got to the back door to go out. When she did exit the door as usual, she immediately ran down the hill as if to attack someone or something. As I walked out behind her, I lit the area up with my hand-held spotlight. I usually spot deer out there, so as to see if a bear or deer or whatever could be upsetting her, but I'm really scared, I'm 54 years of age. I saw what looked to me to be two small, about 4-foot-high beings, made of a light that was faint but only around their head and hand areas, like [their bodies] *were being cloaked by a suit or something. Not really bright, but it is dark out there. They went quickly about ten feet down the hill and what was unreal is they had to lean up and kinda crawl into this opening, like they were going into and up into a craft that had no shape or color. The only way I can describe it was like a portal window or opening a door, but didn't emanate any light source, it's like the craft had a camo-cloaking system or something. But you could tell it was a craft, because when it started to move away from the place it was sitting, about 2* [feet] *off the ground it moved the trees and caused an air turbulence. And as it moved you couldn't see it, but you couldn't see through it or what was behind it, kind of like a shadow moving. I tried to spotlight it, but the craft just absorbed my light. As it moved away it began to rise up into the sky and then you could make out a shape, like I'm really freaked out, they looked back toward me as they entered their craft. Their eyes had a light the color of blue, a pale soft glowing emanating about their eyes, but no face could be recognizable, but they were beings not of this realm. My dog just sat down and did nothing, she stopped barking, and they left. The shape was like a spear head shaped object about 20* [feet] *long and pointed and narrow and wider at the rear.*

January 31, 2008

Opened my front door, and to my surprise, hovering just above the trees I saw something that was very wide, 2 lights in the middle, and one light on each of the wings. Large lights. NO SOUND AT ALL. I closed the door, and had my daughter come to the door and check to make sure that I wasn't a nut, and she saw the same thing. Very scary. We closed the door and went back to the patio door, just in time to see this object leaving. Very wide, and one large light in the back middle portion of this thing. Still heard no noise. This thing was just above the top of the trees, so it was very close. Was low enough to shine the lights into [the] house.

November 17, 2012

Taking place in Stafford, VA from approximately 6:33 P.M. until 6:36 P.M., there were roughly eight to ten very bright luminous orange balls of light in the sky. Traveling at a constant and steady speed, many of them broke off into groups and continued to travel in separate directions until just disappearing without a trace. For a brief moment, they appeared stationary but as they became more visible it was obvious that they were traveling at a considerable speed. Way faster than a helicopter, but it made absolutely no sound. It was clearly in sight and would have made [a] sound if it were a familiar object but remained silent and clearly visible until disappearing one by one. Some appeared to be very close to each other, almost touching but moved uniformly and at a steady speed. Appearing in different groups and formations, the bright orange lights stretched across the sky traveling some in the same direction and some in different directions all traveling from the Northeast. All of them gradually disappeared heading Southwest. [I] checked the local weather immediately after and [the] visibility was 10 miles 46 degrees wind northeast 4 mph (ground level).

August 1, 2018

About a year and a half ago at 2:30 am, I woke up and heard helicopters. I looked out my window and saw a huge triangle craft about the size of a 747, with only one light on the front it was slowly moving across the sky very low. I soon realized the noise was not coming from the object but the 2 choppers following it. I live very close to the Quantico Marine Base in Virginia. It only lasted about 15-20 seconds. My wife would not wake up, so she never saw it. I told her about it the next morning. I'm only disclosing this in case someone else might have reported it. It could help corroborate another sighting. What I saw was amazing and NOT normal.

SPOTSYLVANIA COUNTY

September 1, 1979

Returning home from an evening shopping trip my husband spotted several bright lights in the sky [in] the distance. Instead of continuing through the city to our home, he turned back and headed towards the lights, which made our journey home through the country roads.

What we saw were about 8 and sometimes more very large round lights following the south side of Mine Rd. As we drove beside and watched them, trying to figure out what they were, we began to notice that some would suddenly go dark while another would light up nearby. They all stayed fairly close together and they continued their path directly beside us.

We turned left on Landsdowne Rd, and they also turned with us. Landsdowne Rd is several miles long, so we drove [slowly] and observed. They stayed beside us. We had no preconceptions about UFO's; therefore, we did not feel any threat from this, just curiosity.

Suddenly a helicopter appeared in the sky on the north side of the road. When we heard the helicopter's engine and saw the small light in comparison, we realized that the lights that we had been following (or following us) made absolutely no sound.

When we turned right on the next road my husband decided to keep past our development and go as far as the small airport to see if that was their destination. They continued beside us and on past the airport. This seemed to be a never-ending journey and we were beginning to feel a little strange about it, so we turned around back to our house, which was just a few blocks off the main road. We could still see them behind us, and they seemed to be hovering.

Once home, my son went to get his friend to tell him about this. They climbed on the garage [roof] to see if they could see them. The lights or whatever it was had crossed the road into a large unpopulated area next to our development. My son and his friend watched them hover in that area until they got tired and came in. Of course, I had no fear then about abduction, etc. because I wasn't aware of such things. Today, I would not have taken it so lightly.

August 25, 2015

Single steady, bright emerald, green light viewed through 10" telescope and with naked eye.

I was preparing to photograph the moon, using a 10" SCT telescope, looking through the eyepiece to ensure the moon was centered before attaching the camera. A round, bright, emerald, green light flashed [through] the eyepiece, left to right.

I asked my husband, "What was THAT?", he looked up and saw a single green light slightly above us and to our southwest. I also observed the light without the scope. We immediately dismissed it as an aircraft as we are on the flight path for DC airports, as well as frequent overflights of private aircraft, military aircraft, helicopters, and high-altitude commercial aircraft. In retrospect, however, we realized virtually every passing aircraft has strobing lights, whereas this light was steady.

Later, we deliberately observed aircraft on different nights and indeed all exhibited clearly strobing lights, normally red and/or white. At no time did we observe any aircraft exhibiting a single bright green light.

We have also frequently observed satellites passing overhead, and this bore no resemblance to them, nor was its behavior or speed anything like meteors we have often observed.

We have been intermittently involved in amateur astronomy for close to 30 years and admit, we are skeptical of most UFO reports (not that there is life in the universe, just knowing the distance to even the closest stars would require far more advanced civilizations to overcome the distance and time).

Conditions at the time: partly cloudy, rural location with some horizon sky glow.

November 25, 2017

Orange illuminated sphere close to tree line, moving purposefully across the sky.

Camping at Lake Anna State Park. A large orb of orange light caught my attention as it entered my field of vision. Its speed, size, and color were all unlike any other sky object I've seen.

The more I watched it travel across the sky, the more uneasy I felt about it. It moved across the sky horizontally, not far above the tree line, with very visible up and down jerks—almost like course overcorrections. There were no flashing lights, and it remained the same steady rusty orange color the whole time. It was moving quickly and maintained a constant speed. It moved upwards a little (seemingly intentionally, not the small jerks like earlier) toward the end of its path, and then disappeared behind the tree line.

Spent about 5 minutes watching it cross the sky.

15

BIGFOOT SIGHTING

The existence of a primate native to North America has long been a subject of fascination and speculation. Despite arguments from primatologists that the forests of North America cannot possibly support a primate, people have been seeing strange, hairy beings that resemble a giant ape for decades. Dubbed Bigfoot by the press in the 1950s, this creature has been seen throughout the country, including in Virginia. Sightings of Bigfoot in Virginia are mainly reported in the western part of the state and in the Shenandoah Valley, but there was an intriguing sighting report to the Bigfoot Field Researchers Organization (BFRO) that occurred in Stafford County.

On the evening of September 13, 2003, the witness and his thirteen-year-old daughter were driving on Widewater Road just south of Quantico Marine Corps Base. It was just after dusk, and the witness had turned on his vehicle's headlights. The witness was going about forty miles per hour and was driving through a wooded area. He had just come around a bend when he caught sight of an animal standing in the road. As his headlights lit up the animal, the man and his daughter realized that the creature was large and very hairy. It stood on both legs and to the man appeared to be about seven and a half to eight feet tall, though his daughter later asserted that it appeared to be about six to seven feet tall.

The creature was in the process of crossing the road and had paused when the man's car approached. As the witness slowed down his car, the creature turned its head to look at the witness. At this point, the man's daughter became aware that something was in the road. By this time the creature was standing directly in front of the vehicle. The creature was only thirty feet away from the witness's vehicle. After a few seconds, the creature turned and walked on both legs south into the woods. At no time during the sighting did the creature drop down and walk on four legs. Despite being unsure of what they had just witnessed, they would both assert to an BFRO investigator that the creature was not a bear.

Both witnesses saw that the animal was completely covered in dark brown, matted hair. To the man, when the creature paused and looked at him, it felt like a deliberate act, as if the creature was checking them out. The man felt that there was a substantial presence to the animal that he did not feel looking into the eyes of a bear or deer. At no time did the animal appear to be frightened of the man or the vehicle and crossed the street in a determined but casual manner. While the man was fascinated by what he was witnessing, the man's daughter was so terrified that she could not clearly focus on what she was seeing. According to the witness, this was not the first time that he had witnessed a creature that he believed was Bigfoot. The investigator for BFRO who analyzed the man's report was impressed with what was reported and gave this sighting a Class A rating on the BFRO database. A Class A sighting is a report that involved a clear sighting of a Bigfoot where misidentification of common animals can be ruled out.

BIBLIOGRAPHY

ARTICLES

Aubrecht, Michael. "Bernard Slave Cabins." Emerging Civil War, https:// emergingcivilwar.com.

Blackford, Charles M. "Four Successive John Minors (Concluded)." *Virginia Magazine of History and Biography* 10, no. 4 (April 1903): 436–40.

Chasen, Donna. "Hazel Hill: Splendor of the Past." *Fredericksburg (VA) Free Lance-Star*, August 14, 2004. https://fredericksburg.com.

Farkas, Harold M. "The V.I.P. Ghosts in Virginia: A Spectral Who's Who." *New York Times*, January 24, 1971.

Fore, Samuel K. "George Augustine Washington (ca. 1759–1793)." George Washington's Mount Vernon, www.mountvernon.org.

———. "Hugh Mercer." George Washington's Mount Vernon, www. mountvernon.org.

Haulman, Kate. "The Mother of the Father: Memorializing Mary Washington in Antebellum Virginia." In *Women in George Washington's World*, edited by Charlene M. Boyer and George Boudreau, 19–42. Charlottesville: University of Virginia Press, 2002.

Henderson, Malanna. "Defending the New Nation: The Fredericksburg Gun Manufacturing Plant." Emerging Revolutionary War Era, November 14, 2016. https://emergingrevolutionarywar.org.

Hennessy, John. "Digging Mannsfield." *Mysteries & Conundrums*, December 3, 2010. https://npsfrsp.wordpress.com.

Jett, Cathy. "Rising Sun Tavern to Highlight Ghostly Prankster on John Frazer Night." *Fredericksburg (VA) Free Lance-Star*, October 26, 2017. https://fredericksburg.com.

Johnson, Rebecca A. "Betty Washington Lewis." George Washington's Mount Vernon, www.mountvernon.org.

Pfanz, Donald. "Burying the Dead at Spotsylvania—1864." *Mysteries & Conundrums*, April 4, 2011. https://npsfrsp.wordpress.com.

———. "Martha Stephens: Heroine or Hoax?" *Fredericksburg (VA) Free-Lance Star*, July 28, 2001. https://fredericksburg.com.

———. "'Skeleton Hunt'—Spotsylvania 1865." *Mysteries & Conundrums*, April 11, 2011. https://npsfrsp.wordpress.com.

Quinton, Rebecca. "A Virginian Merchant's Waistcoat." *Glasgow Life*, February 15, 2022. https://www.glasgowlife.org.uk.

Richmond (VA) Enquirer, June 12, 1816.

———. June 15, 1816.

Treesh, Catherine. "Committees of Correspondence." George Washington's Mount Vernon, www.mountvernon.org.

Vierick, Scott. "Charles Washington (1738–1799)." George Washington's Mount Vernon, www.mountvernon.org.

Virginia Gazette (Williamsburg, VA). August 23, 1776 (supplement), pg. 1.

———. Purdie and Dixon: December 2, 1773, 2.

———. Rind and Pinkney: December 23, 1775, 3.

———. Dixon and Hunter: February 21, 1777, 1.

Washington Heritage Museums. "Hugh Mercer Apothecary Shop: History of 1020 Caroline Street," *Training Manual for Interpreters*, 2019, Section 5.2: 1-2.

———. "Hugh Mercer Apothecary Shop: Hugh Mercer Biography." *Training Manual for Interpreters*, Section 5.1., 1–2. Fredericksburg, VA: Washington Heritage Museums, 2019.

———. "Rising Sun Tavern: Charles Washington Biography," *Training Manual for Interpreters*, 2019, Section 6.1: 1-2.

———. "Rising Sun Tavern: History of the Rising Sun Tavern," *Training Manual for Interpreters*, 2019, Section 6.2: 1-3.

White, Kristopher D. "Horror and Heroism at the Slaughter Pen Farm." American Battlefield Trust, December 8, 2017. www.battlefields.org.

BOOKS

Alvey, Edward, Jr. *The Fredericksburg Fire of 1807*. Fredericksburg, VA: Historic Fredericksburg Foundation, 1988.

Blackford, L. Minor. *Mine Eyes Have Seen the Glory*. Cambridge, MA: Harvard University Press, 1954.

Brown, Beth. *Haunted Plantations of Virginia*. Atglen, PA: Schiffer Publishing Ltd., 2009.

Felder, Paula S. *Fielding Lewis and the Washington Family: A Chronicle of 18th Century Fredericksburg*. Fredericksburg, VA: American History Company, 1998.

————. *George Washington's Fredericksburg*. Virginia Beach, VA: Donning Company Publishers, 1988, 2011.

George Washington's Ferry Farm & Historic Kenmore Interpreters Handbook. Fredericksburg, VA: George Washington Foundation, n.d.

Goodwin, David, and Troy Taylor. *Soldiers and the Supernatural: America's Haunted Forts, Prisons, Battlefields and Military Ghosts*. Decatur, IL: Whitechapel Press, 2013.

Hamilton, Michelle L. *Mary Ball Washington: The Mother of George Washington*. Ruther Glen, VA: MLH Publications, 2017.

————. *Virginia's Haunted History*. Queenstown, MD: Haunted Road Media, 2022.

Harland, Marion. *The Story of Mary Washington*. Boston: Houghton, Mifflin and Company, 1893.

Helton, Cindy, Malanna Henderson, Steward Henderson, Craig Rains and Trip Wiggins. *A Brief History of St. George's Episcopal Church*. Fredericksburg, VA: St. George's Episcopal Church, 2023.

Lancaster, Robert A., Jr. *Historic Virginia Homes and Churches*. Philadelphia: J.B. Lippincott Company, 1915.

Lee, Marguerite Dupont. *Virginia Ghosts*. Berryville: Virginia Book Company, 1966.

Janney, Caroline E. *Burying the Dead Not the Past: Ladies' Memorial Associations & the Lost Cause*. Chapel Hill: University of North Carolina Press, 2008.

Maloy, Mark. *Victory or Death: The Battles of Trenton and Princeton, December 25, 1776–January 3, 1777*. El Dorado Hills, CA: Savas Beatie LLC, 2018.

Marler, Helen R. *The History and Haunting Stories of Fredericksburg, Virginia*. Westminster, MD: Heritage Books, 2008.

Nesbitt, Mark. *Civil War Ghost Trails: Stories from America's Most Haunted Battlefields*. Mechanicsburg, PA: Stackpole Books, 2012.

————. *Cursed in Virginia: Stories of the Damned in the Old Dominion State.* Guildford, CT: Globe Pequot, 2017.

Pfanz, Donald C. *Fredericksburg: A Comprehensive Civil War Guide.* Privately published, 2022.

Pirok, Alena. *The Spirit of Colonial Williamsburg: Ghosts and Interpreting the Recreated Past.* Amherst, MA: University of Boston Press, 2022.

Quenzel, Carrol H. *The History and Background of St. George's Episcopal Church Fredericksburg, Virginia.* Richmond, VA: Clyde W. Saunders and Sons, 1951.

Riley, Edward Miles. *The Journal of John Harrower: An Indentured Servant in the Colony of Virginia 1773–1776.* Williamsburg, VA: Colonial Williamsburg, 1963.

Sale, Edith Tunis. *Manors of Virginia in Colonial Times.* Philadelphia: J.B. Lippincott Company, 1909.

Taylor, L.B., Jr. *The Ghosts of Fredericksburg…and Nearby Environs.* Williamsburg, VA: Progress Printing Co., Inc., 1991.

WEBSITES

American Battlefield Trust. "Fredericksburg Battle Facts and Summary." Accessed March 31, 2024, https://www.battlefields.org/learn/civil-war/battles/fredericksburg.

————. "Fredericksburg: Confederate Victory, Union Story." Accessed March 31, 2024, https://www.battlefields.org/learn/articles/fredericksburg-0.

————. "Spotsylvania Court House Battle Facts and Summary." Accessed February 27, 2024, https://www.battlefields.org/learn/civil-war/battles/spotsylvania-court-house.

————. "Spotsylvania Court House: Hell Defined, May 8-21, 1864." Accessed February 27, 2024, https://www.battlefields.org/learn/articles/spotsylvania-court-house-hell-defined.

Ancestry.com. "Henry Mitchell." U.S. and Canda, Passenger and Immigration Lists Index, 1500s–1900s. Accessed March 6, 2024, https://www.ancestry.com/discoveryui-content/view/962022:7486?tid=&pid=&queryId=9bbc7f99-afa7-4f3f-8301-fb1f647eac0d&_phsrc=iHu46&_phstart=successSource.

Belle Grove Plantation. "History of a Southern Plantation." Accessed February 24, 2024, https://www.bellegroveplantation.com/history/.

Bigfoot Field Research Organization. "Report #679 Class A." Accessed March 24, 2024, https://www.bfro.net/GDB/show_report.asp?id=679.

———. "Report #30258 Class A." Accessed March 24, 2024, https://www.bfro.net/GDB/show_report.asp?id=30258.

———. "Report #34337 Class B." Accessed March 24, 2024, https://www.bfro.net/GBD/show_report.asp?id=34337.

Encyclopedia Virginia. "Fielding Lewis (1725-1781 or 1782)." Accessed March 25, 2024, https://encyclopediavirginia.org/entries/lewis-fielding-1725-1781-or-1782/.

Find A Grave. "Christian Brown Graham." Accessed February 25, 2024, https://www.findagrave.com/memorial/17047946/christian-graham.

———. "Col. Gustavus Brown Wallace." Accessed March 1, 2024, https://www.findagrave.com/memorial/5095936/gustavus-brown-wallace/.

———. "Dr. Hugh McDonald Martin." Accessed March 25, 2024, https://www.findagrave.com/memorial/5137988/hugh-mcdonald-martin.

———. "Hugh Mercer." Accessed March 23, 2024, https://www.findagrave.com/memorial/2677/hugh-mercer.

———. "Gen. John Minor." Accessed February 23, 2024, https://www.findagrave.com/memorial/5041205/john-minor.

———. "Mary Nelson Berkely Minor." Accessed February 23, 2024, https://www.findagrave.com/memorial/31376453/mary_nelson_minor.

Fredericksburg, Stafford, Spotsylvania Historical Markers. "Brig. Gen. John Minor n-32." Accessed February 23, 2024. https://fredmarkers.umwblogs.org/2008/03/23/brig-gen-john-minor-n-32/.

George Washington Foundation. "About the George Washington Foundation." Accessed March 28, 2024. https://kenmore.org/about-the-foundation/.

Happy Retreat. "Charles Washington." Accessed March 3, 2024, https://www.happyretreat.org/history/charles-washington/.

National Park Service. "Chatham Slave Revolt." Accessed March 31, 2024. https://www.nps.gov/frsp/learn/historyculture/chatham-slave-revolt.htm.

National UFO Reporting Center. "NUFORC Sighting 42529." Accessed February 20, 2024. https://nuforc.org/sighting/?id=42529.

———. "NUFORC Sighting 58429." Accessed February 20, 2024. https://nuforc.org/sighting/?id=58429.

———. "NUFORC Sighting 61414." Accessed February 20, 2024. https://nuforc.org/sighting/?id=61414.

———. "NUFORC Sighting 80571." Accessed February 20, 2024. https://nuforc.org/sighting/?id=80571.

———. "NUFORC Sighting 82692." Accessed February 20, 2024. https://nuforc.org/sighting/?id=82692.

———. "NUFORC Sighting 94573." Accessed February 20, 2024. https://nuforc.org/sighting/?id=94573.

———. "NUFORC Sighting 121563." Accessed February 20, 2024. https://nuforc.org/sighting/?id=121563.

———. "NUFORC Sighting 129253." Accessed February 20, 2024. https://nuforc.org/sighting/?id=129253.

———. "NUFORC Sighting 131938." Accessed February 20, 2024. https://nuforc.org/sighting/?id=131938.

———. "NUFORC Sighting 132556." Accessed February 20, 2024. https://nuforc.org/sighting/?id=132556.

———. "NUFORC Sighting 137458." Accessed February 20, 2024. https://nuforc.org/sighting/?id=137458.

———. "NUFORC Sighting 136592." Accessed February 20, 2024. https://nuforc.org/sighting/?id=136592.

———. "NUFORC Sighting 158690." Accessed February 20, 2024. https://nuforc.org/sighting/?id=158690.

———. "NUFORC Sighting 160808." Accessed February 20, 2024. https://nuforc.org/sighting/?id=160808.

———. "NUFORC Sighting 170872." Accessed February 20, 2024. https://nuforc.org/sighting/?id=170872.

———. "NUFORC Sighting 171436." Accessed February 20, 2024. https://nuforc.org/sighting/?id=171436.

———. "NUFORC Sighting 175105." Accessed February 20, 2024. https://nuforc.org/sighting/?id=175105.

———. "NUFORC Sighting 175127." Accessed February 20, 2024. https://nuforc.org/sighting/?id=175127.

St. George's History. "Dr. Brodie Strachan Herndon (1810–1886)." Accessed March 20, 2024. https://history.churchsp.org/dr-brodie-strachan-herndon-1810-1886/.

———. "Ghosts of St. George's— 'The Gentle Ghost.'" Accessed March 25, 2024. https://history.churchsp.org/the-gentle-ghost-of-st-georges/.

US Ghost Adventures. "The Haunted Aquia Church." Accessed February 25, 2024. https://usghostadventures.com/haunted-stories/americas-most-haunted-east/the-haunted-aquia-church/.

Virginia Museum of History & Culture. "Kenmore." Accessed March 28, 2024. https://virginiahistory.org/research/collections/garden-club-virginia-historic-restorations-project/house-sites/kenmore.

Wikipedia. "Betty Washington Lewis." Accessed March 25, 2024. https://en.wikipedia.org/wiki/Betty_Washington_Lewis.

———. "Chatham Manor." Accessed March 31, 2024. https://en.wikipedia.org/wiki/Chatham_Manor.

———. "The Chimneys (Fredericksburg, Virginia)." Accessed March 13, 2024. https://en.wikipedia.org/wiki/The_Chimneys_(Fredericksburg,_Virginia).

———. "Committee of Safety (American Revolution)." Accessed February 28, 2024. https://en.wikipedia.org/wiki/Committee_of_safety_(American_Revolution).

———. "Fielding Lewis." Accessed March 25, 2024. https://en.wikipedia.org/wiki/Fielding_Lewis.

———. "George Dashiell Bayard." Accessed February 24, 2024. https://en.wikipedia.org/wiki/George_Dashiell_Bayard.

———. "George Weedon." Accessed March 23, 2024. https://en.wikipedia.org/wiki/George_Weedon.

———. "Hugh Mercer." Accessed March 23, 2024. https://en.wikipedia.org/wiki/Hugh_Mercer.

———. "Jacobite Rising of 1745." Accessed March 23, 2024. https://en.wikipedia.org/wiki/Jacobite_rising_of_1745.

———. "Joan, Lady John Campbell." Accessed March 13, 2024. https://en.wikipedia.org/wiki/Joan,_Lady_John_Campbell.

———. "Kenmore (Fredericksburg, Virginia)," Accessed March 25, 2024. https://en.wikipedia.org/wiki/Kenmore_(Fredericksburg,_Virginia).

———. "Mann Page." Accessed February 24, 2024. https://en.wikipedia.org/wiki/Mann_Page.

Wythepedia: The George Wythe Encyclopedia. "John Minor." Accessed February 23, 2024. https://lawlibrary.wm.edu/wythepedia/index.php/John_Minor.

ABOUT THE AUTHOR

M ichelle L. Hamilton earned her master's degree in history from San Diego State University. Hamilton is the author or editor of several books, including *"I Would Still Be Drowned in Tears": Spiritualism in Abraham Lincoln's White House, Mary Ball Washington: The Mother of George Washington* and *Civil War Ghosts*. She has also published articles in *The Morbid Curious* and *The Feminine Macabre*. Hamilton has worked as a docent at several museums across the county, including the Whaley House in San Diego, California. She is currently the manager of the Mary Washington House in Fredericksburg, Virginia. Hamilton lives in Caroline County, Virginia, with her family and three spoiled poodles. A passionate fan of the TV series *Doctor Who*, in her free time she is a panelist on *The Sense Sphere* on YouTube.

FREE eBOOK OFFER

Scan the QR code below, enter your e-mail address and get our original Haunted America compilation eBook delivered straight to your inbox for free.

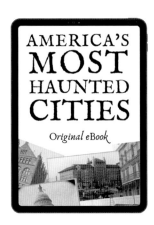

ABOUT THE BOOK

Every city, town, parish, community and school has their own paranormal history. Whether they are spirits caught in the Bardo, ancestors checking on their descendants, restless souls sending a message or simply spectral troublemakers, ghosts have been part of the human tradition from the beginning of time.

In this book, we feature a collection of stories from five of America's most haunted cities: Baltimore, Chicago, Galveston, New Orleans and Washington, D.C.

SCAN TO GET
AMERICA'S MOST HAUNTED CITIES

Having trouble scanning? Go to:
biz.arcadiapublishing.com/americas-most-haunted-cities